yogalates

The breakthrough workout that
combines the best of
Yoga and Pilates

Louise Solomon

STERLING PUBLISHING CO., INC.
NEW YORK

PUBLISHER'S ACKNOWLEDGEMENTS
Design: Smith & Gilmour
Commissoned photography: Tim Hazel
Models: Crystal Solomon-LeBars; Amber Parry
Illustrations: Michael Travers
Thanks to Deborah Dooley for her creative writing contribution

Library of Congress Cataloging-in-Publication Data Available
10 9 8 7 6 5 4 3 2 1

Published in 2003 by Sterling Publishing Co., Inc.
387 Park Avenue South
New York, NY 10016

First published in Great Britain in 2003 by Virgin Books Ltd.
Thames Wharf Studios
Rainville Road, London, W6 9HA
© Louise Solomon 2003

Distributed in Canada by Sterling Publishing
C/o Canadian Manda Group
One Atlantic Avenue, Suite 105
Toronto, Ontario, M6K 3E7, Canada

Printed in Great Britain by Butler and Tanner

Sterling ISBN 1-4027-0713-4

It is always important to consult your doctor before commencing an exercise program, especially if you have a medical condition or are pregnant. All guidelines and warnings should be heeded. The author and publisher disclaim any liability or loss, personal or otherwise, resulting from the procedures and information contained in this book.

Contents

Dedication

I dedicate this book

To my daughter Crystal, my husband Mark. I would not be the person
I am today without their love, friendship, support of my vision and above
all their sacrifice of our family time to the creation of Yogalates.

To my parents and family for their love and support.

To the Yoga gurus of the east who brought Yoga to the west enlightening
us with their presence, knowledge and teachings.

To Joseph Pilates for his revolutionary vision of bodywork that inspired me.

To all my students and clients from the Suffolk Park Hall where Yogalates
originated many years ago. Through them I have grown, my work has
flourished and they have taught me so much more than they will ever know.

And to the evolution of nature and science, through the existence of the
human body, mind and spirit. That still fires my passion today.

With total gratitude and love

   Namaste

   Louise

Health Guidance

Some exercises are not suitable for everyone. If you are unsure about
this exercise program, please consult your doctor first.

Foreword

When I first discovered Yogalates I was suffering with repetitive strain syndrome in both wrists. As a physiotherapist, I was unable to fulfill my role satisfactorily, and subsequently felt ineffective and purposeless. I hadn't realized just how entwined and interdependent my physical injury and my self-confidence were. I started a regular Yogalates practice, and after each one I would come away with something new. The benefits amassed continue to affect my life in a profound way.

Louise Solomon is an inspiration. She has created a truly unique method, which is always evolving and adapting to reflect the most recent scientific research, making this knowledge accessible to the general public in a safe, practical and enjoyable way. Yogalates helps you re-educate your body in the way it moves. It places you inside your body and restores strength, posture and movement systematically, gradually repairing the years of neglect, abuse and bad habits.

This is where your journey begins. I wish you all the best as you travel the road to holistic health, happiness and wellbeing.

Anna Michel
Bachelor of Physiotherapy, MAPA

Chapter 1

Yogalates – Origins and History

Most of us know that the key to successful exercising is to find the right workout for you. One that becomes a part of your life that you don't want to do without, and which gives you the kind of results we all want. I believe that like so many others – myself included – your search for the perfect exercise system ends here, with your discovery of Yogalates. Why? Because Yogalates combines the very best of two historically and widely acclaimed exercise systems, Yoga and Pilates. A perfect fusion of East meeting West, which improves overall health, strengthens tones and beautifies the body, and brings quiet, calm and peace to the mind.

Through my own extensive professional experience with both Yoga and Pilates I have developed a union of these two brilliant art forms, bringing you an innovative system of exercise – and an opportunity to achieve the ultimate exercise goal, a strong healthy body and a strong centered mind. If you practice Yogalates three times a week for a month you'll see an incredible difference in the way you move, look and feel. And after three months, not only will Yogalates have changed your life to the point where you'll never want to give it up – you'll also have created the body you've always wanted.

Yoga has always been a favourite form of exercise of mine, because as well as being a great way to strengthen and tone the body, it has excellent therapeutic value for calming the mind and spirit. Yoga originated around 3,000 BC and has a deep and profound history of bestowing physical and emotional wellbeing, as millions of people all over the world can testify. It exercises the body and increases flexibility while focusing the mind on the movement in a meditative way, which many people find very spiritual. The emphasis is on muscle sensations and relaxed breathing, and using the *asanas* (postures) and the *pranayama* (breath) to restore a healthy balance of nerves, circulation, hormones and digestion. It is this holistic approach which makes Yoga an invaluable aid to general health and overall wellbeing. Twelve years ago I turned to Yoga for relief from stress and general burnout through overwork. It helped my recovery immensely, but sadly, a lack of training and proper instruction in my Yoga class led me to attempt postures I wasn't yet ready for. As a result, I developed a serious groin injury and the resulting pain meant that I had to give up practicing Yoga.

Disillusioned, I looked around for an alternative form of exercise, and discovered that a friend had got rid of her back pain for the first time in years

by practicing an exercise system called Pilates (pronounced pee-lah-tees). That was the beginning of my love affair with Pilates and, for the next two and a half years, it was my sole form of exercise.

So what makes Pilates special? For me it's the fact that this is a system of physical training which has been developed and honoured for years – a tried and true formula, now taught throughout the world, with nine decades of success behind it. Like the bodies it seeks to improve, the Pilates system has been honed and toned over the decades, to make it more streamlined and efficient. But the original philosophy of its inventor, Joseph Pilates, remains true today – to re-educate the body and focus on training both mind and body towards a goal of overall fitness. Joseph Pilates was a man ahead of his time and it's our great good fortune that we can benefit so much from his original concept and beliefs about how a healthy body works. With exceptional body awareness he knew instinctively that when the stomach muscles were pulled firmly back to the spine, the lower back was supported, making it strong and safe from injury.

The best way of understanding Pilates is by comparing it to an apple. Pilates focuses on the apple core. It's designed to increase the strength of the deep postural muscles (known as core stability), thereby lessening the risk of injury. Dancers love Pilates for its lengthening streamlining effects, and after a few months of regularly practicing Pilates, I could see exactly why. I began to feel taller, slimmer and as if I weighed less! My new-found strength (core stability) seemed to come from within, giving me wonderful posture, graceful fluid movements and great muscle tone – which translated into an overall leaner shape. During the next two and a half years, I went on to train and teach Pilates, but although I loved what I was doing, I missed the therapeutic value of Yoga, and the meditative quality of the classes. So I returned to train in Yoga, learning more about its concepts, and it was then that I began to see how Pilates could be integrated with Yoga, to create a fusion of both worlds.

Yogalates is the modern form of Yoga for the Western body. The classic Indian lifestyle is very different from ours, in that they spend much of their leisure time squatting or sitting on the ground instead of sitting on chairs and sofas. We in the West, however, are often desk-bound from a young age, and the era of the computer has itself been very detrimental for our bodies and health in general. Our sedentary lives mean that our bodies are not conditioned for extreme Yogic postures, making us vulnerable to injury. This is where Yogalates comes in – bridging the gap between Eastern and Western forms of exercise. The support that my idea received from professional practitioners, as well as people eager to attend classes, convinced me that I wasn't the only one who saw the enormous potential of this idea. The Yogalates journey had begun.

I spent the next decade exploring, creating and developing my work in my own studio. I travelled throughout the USA and the UK experiencing and studying Yoga and Pilates.

Yogalates is a movement system which originally started by simply incorporating the best of the Yoga and Pilates worlds, but in conjunction with the latest medical research, it has developed and evolved further. A combination of anatomy and physiology has been used to devise and refine a set of safe, controlled and extraordinarily effective exercises, putting Yogalates at the leading edge of health and fitness.

The Pilates concept of drawing the stomach muscles to the spine is supported by current literature, and has proved to be a simplified version of the much more complex support system of the human body. However, instead of the machines used in Pilates, Yogalates uses physiotherapy exercise bands to build and lengthen muscles and maintain bone density, protecting you from the onset of osteoporosis. And, acknowledging updated medical knowledge – and because the Yogalates method views the human body holistically – I have taken the concept of core stability one step further, by increasing the strength and stability of the muscles closest to the whole of the skeleton, with the 'Yogalates girdles'. These girdles encompass the deep postural muscles of the spine and pelvis, which all work in unison, and by focusing to this extent on core stability, correct posture is enhanced – in turn supporting the nervous system running along our very core (spine). So when we exercise our spine we also rejuvenate the nervous system – vital in ensuring the healthy function of muscles and organs and encouraging the entire body to work in balance. In Yogalates there is also heightened focus on the pelvic floor muscles and their important role as a stable platform at the base of the pelvis. These muscles act as a support mechanism and an aid to bowel and bladder function, and it really does pay to keep them strong – as any woman who's given birth will tell you!

Yogalates is strenuous but safe, stretching and strengthening all the major muscle groups and deeper muscles, enhancing posture and developing slenderness rather than bulk – which in turn helps you to achieve that coveted streamlined shape. Flexibility and grace are coaxed and encouraged through the use of controlled twisting movements, incorporating the spiritual moves of Yoga, and dynamic Yogic breathing, which unblocks and balances energy, and tones internal organs.

As you've probably guessed, all this doesn't happen overnight, but the real beauty of Yogalates is that by practicing it consistently, you will gain a real understanding and appreciation of your body – how it works and moves. Above all, at a time when the fitness industry is falling over itself to create new and ever more gimmicky trends, Yogalates is an intensely practical system of rejuvenating, restructuring, reducing and toning your body, as well as preventing the onset of back pain and lowering stress levels. There are no quick fixes, but with perseverance you will learn techniques which will help you make the most of basic posture and movement, and completely change the way you go through daily life – walking, running, lifting and playing sport.

So if you want a flatter belly, a trimmer waist, and a streamlined and beautifully toned shape, not to mention more strength and stamina, better health, and a sense of inner calm and wellbeing – start practicing Yogalates today. All you need is some basic equipment, a few hours a week, and a determination to become the person you've always wanted to be.

Chapter 2

Body Basics

I've always found that students who have a basic grasp of anatomy – a good understanding of how the body works – get the most benefit out of any exercise program. Because they know all the whys and wherefores, they can really focus on each muscle as it works, concentrating on making sure that each exercise is done correctly, precisely and in a way that achieves maximum results. It's equally important to have an understanding of the internal function of the body, which is incredibly intricate in its design and, although delicate, is also unbelievably resilient.

The complexity of the human body never ceases to amaze and impress me, but for the sake of simplicity we'll divide it into seven basic systems – remembering that the overall health and optimal function of the body is dependent on the interplay of all of these systems. So, they are: the *musculo-skeletal system* – that's muscles and bones; the *respiratory system* – concerning the lungs; the *cardiovascular* – the heart and major arteries; the *lymphatic* – to do with immunity; the *visceral* – major organs in the body; the *endocrine system* – circulation of hormones; and the *central nervous system* – which connects the mind and body and is responsible for keeping all the above working well!

So let's first take a look at the ***musculo-skeletal system*** – responsible for movement, posture, and, very importantly, protecting the internal organs. Your skeleton is the framework of your body and is made up of bones that are actually complex tissues. The function of the bones is to support the body's tissues and organs, provide attachment sites for muscles, and store essential minerals which are important for muscle contraction and nerve activity. Blood cells are produced within the bone marrow and released into the circulation.

Each of the joints in your skeleton is controlled by a group of muscles called the flexors, which bend the muscles, and the extensors, which straighten them. Some joints also have rotator muscles which turn, twist and rotate the bones; e.g. the head, neck, hips, wrists and ankles. Muscles are responsible for holding the skeleton upright, and they provide motion, maintain posture and generate heat. Although the size of your muscles isn't important, their condition is. This means making sure that the muscle groups controlling a joint are balanced – of equal strength, and therefore less prone to damage or injury. Exercise strengthens the bones, keeping them healthy and slowing the ageing process, but it's the muscles which generate and control movement, by pulling on the tendons attached to the bones. Think of it like puppet strings moving parts of the skeleton around. By

selectively stretching and strengthening these different muscle groups within the balanced exercise program of Yogalates, you can realign your posture, get rid of niggling aches and pains, and achieve the kind of muscle tone and definition we all love.

On to the **respiratory system** – responsible for bringing breath and oxygen into the body and eliminating carbon dioxide – which maintains a healthy acid balance in the body. The lungs are housed within the ribcage and work in tandem with the diaphragm (breathing muscle) to control the passage of breath in and out of the body. Movement of the diaphragm massages the stomach and internal organs, contributing to their health and function, and the lungs also help to produce sound, our major means of communication. Exercise promotes correct breathing through the full excursion of the diaphragm and expansion of the ribcage, creating stamina and endurance, and breathing through the nose filters and moistens the air being taken into the body, enriching the blood and renewing body tissue.

Breath is the very essence of the body. We breathe to live – and holding our breath is not helpful. Every time we inhale and exhale, oxygen feeds and pumps through our body, to rejuvenate muscles and carry away toxic waste. The smooth, even breathing that we teach in Yogalates releases tension and creates free-flowing movement.

Now for the **cardiovascular system** – responsible for the circulation of blood around the body, which in turn carries oxygen and nutrients to each and every cell, removing waste products and toxins as it goes. The heart and blood vessels form a complete and very efficient transportation network that does a great job of delivering adequate supplies of oxygen to exercising muscles. The cardiovascular system also carries hormones around the body, regulating their activity and controlling body temperature. As well as strengthening the heart muscles, Yogalates exercises stir a sluggish circulation into action, which has an energizing effect, clearing the mind and firming the will.

The **lymphatic system** is responsible for maintaining a healthy immune system, and it does this by filtering toxins and releasing and circulating cells which fight infection and disease. The power of the body to prevent or resist the disease process depends largely on a lymphatic system that is healthy and in good working order. Yogalates boosts this process, speeding the removal of toxins from the body and triggering the release of 'fighter' cells.

The **visceral system** – responsible for the functioning of the major organs in the body and maintaining life itself – benefits from the flexibility created in Yogalates, which continuously frees blocked nerve passages leading to the organs, boosting metabolism and contributing to their health. The combination of the postures and the dynamic breathing system means that the organs are kept toned and in good condition.

The **endocrine system** – responsible for the production, circulation and regulation of hormones, and maintaining balance throughout the body – controls and integrates functions of other organ systems in the body such as growth, reproduction, digestion and respiration, and also controls the body's response to everyday stresses.

The **central nervous system** (CNS) (see pic below) is responsible for the optimal function and the co-ordination of all the systems of the human body. It connects the mind and body, functioning through cells which communicate via electrical currents that are rapid and specific – usually producing immediate responses, enhancing the quality and control of movement and enabling the body to react to continuous change. Luckily for us, the CNS is incredibly flexible and adaptable and can and will reprogram as needed. It is the master control and communication system of the body – the bridge of the ship, involved with every thought, action, instinct and emotion. The strong mind/body connection developed by the practice of Yogalates, and the calm confidence it fosters, will help your central nervous system keep the whole ship running smoothly.

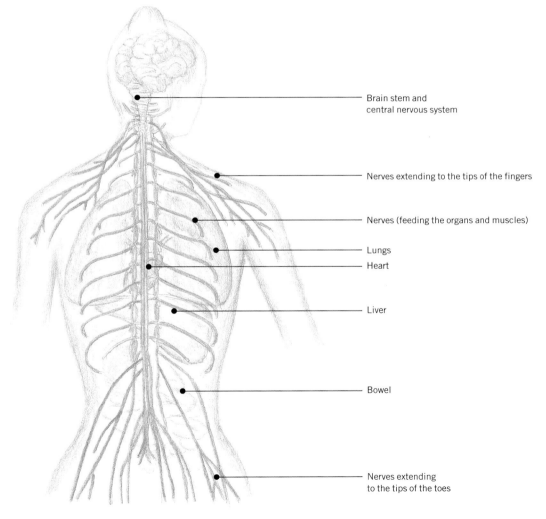

Brain stem and central nervous system

Nerves extending to the tips of the fingers

Nerves (feeding the organs and muscles)

Lungs

Heart

Liver

Bowel

Nerves extending to the tips of the toes

The CNS – The master control center

Why Exercise is Good for You

We all know that exercise is good for us. It's one of the few messages that remains constant, whether we hear it from health professionals, media or government. But despite this, today's lifestyle is much more sedentary than that of previous generations – and this lack of activity is damaging to the spine. As we age, the spine loses its ability to maintain its strong tower-like structure, and in order to absorb nutrients, stay healthy and function well, the spinal discs need to be exercised regularly.

Now let's take a look at exactly what else exercise can do for us in terms of feeling and looking our best. Regular exercise has the effect of improving cardiovascular fitness – i.e. it makes your heart and lungs work more efficiently. It also builds muscular strength and endurance, along with general stamina, makes you flexible, agile and gives you better co-ordination. This all keeps your body in good working order and makes you move gracefully and look taller and slimmer. The improvement in circulation brought on by exercise flushes toxins out of the body, helping you to lose weight and get rid of excess fluid, and makes your skin glow. In addition to this, regular activity and exercises can reduce blood pressure and cholesterol levels, prevent and combat obesity and diabetes, increase bone density, relieve arthritic conditions and reduce stress levels, promoting a general feeling of wellbeing. In short, regular exercise will make you feel and look great.

Sounds good doesn't it? But the key word here is regular. It's widely recognized that to gain maximum benefits, you need to take some form of physical activity three to five times every week, for around twenty to sixty minutes.

'Re-educate your body the way nature intends, keeping the mind and body stress free'

I recommend that, like me, you vary your physical routine by alternating long walks or swims with your Yogalates practice. This cross-training approach to fitness will mean that you never get bored and ensures that you get the maximum physical and mental benefits from exercise. Using the Yogalates band adds the element of resistance to your exercise routine, which has the multiple effect of strengthening the skeleton, increasing the energy expended by the muscles, and taking them through their full range. This means that as the muscles on one side of the joints are strengthened, the ones on the other side are stretched – getting a great balance, toning and helping to shed excess pounds. And all this from one simple band!

When you've established your exercise routine, you'll see that you are retraining areas of the body which have become lax, and learning to reprogram your muscles. In order to do this effectively, with no possibility of injury, it's important to clear your mind of distractions and be really focused on the job in hand. The centering phase, covered later in the book, is invaluable for helping with this. We're going to be working with the aid of diagrams, to train the mind and body to work together towards our goal of overall fitness, and of course this means that you can look forward to getting the kind of body you've always wanted. But a regular exercise program which becomes part of your life is much more than that. I like to think of mine as a long-term maintenance program for my body – keeping me fit and active, helping me look good and increasing my confidence – and ultimately creating independence, vital for ageing with mobility and grace.

Chapter 3
Core Issues

So many people today experience musculo-skeletal problems simply because of their sedentary lifestyle. Sitting still is an unnatural state of affairs – the human body was designed to move around. This adds weight to the notion that exercise is good for us, but it needs to be the right kind of exercise, initiating movement in the right way – exerting physical effort from a stable and centered base. I like to think of this movement as coming from the inside out, and this is actually a key concept in the practice of Yogalates.

Every single Yogalates exercise revolves around what we call the core of the body – the skeleton, spine and pelvis. Like the apple core mentioned in Chapter 1, the core of the body is its very center, providing stability, a solid base from which to work, and guarding against injury. Correct spinal alignment during exercise and movement is vital for protecting and strengthening the spinal column, and promoting optimal health and efficient function of all the body's systems, as well as keeping the internal organs properly aligned and placed. So let's look at the structure which makes up the all-important core of the body, and see how we can best take care of it and help it do its job to the very best of its ability.

We'll start with the spine, which really is the backbone of our existence. Made up of 24 vertebrae, varying in size, these articulate with one another to create a delicately balanced tower of great structural integrity, capable of movement in all directions. In order to ensure correct loading or stacking of vertebra on vertebra – and consequently minimizing the work of the muscles required to maintain upright posture and movement, a healthy spine forms three natural curves which develop as a child grows to adulthood. I call this the neutral spine concept – and I'll be referring to this throughout the book as we go through the Yogalates exercises and discuss the benefits Yogalates will have on your health. So, starting at the bottom of the spine, the first natural curve consists of five vertebrae, which curve towards the front of the body and form the lower back, called the lumbar spine. Moving up the skeleton, the next twelve vertebrae curve towards the back of the body, forming the mid-back, and are called the thoracic spine. And the final natural curve, consisting of seven vertebrae, is the neck, which, like the lumbar spine, curves towards the front of the body. Known as the cervical spine, it supports the weight of the head.

Like the rest of the skeleton, however, the spine has more than one job. As well as supporting the body and its movement, the spine also houses and protects the central nervous system within the spinal column. The CNS runs all the way from the base of the skull down to the beginning of the lumbar

curve. In between each vertebra are the exit points for the spinal nerves. As we've already discovered, no part of the mind or body functions on any level without the CNS. It is constantly sending messages from the skull down to the back of the pelvis, from the brain to the muscles, for control of movement – and in turn, receptors in the muscles send messages back to the brain, regarding quality of movement. So it's easy to see that as well as integrity, elongation and mobility of the spine, space for the spine to 'breathe' is very important – allowing a free flow of these vital messages.

Because the focus of Yogalates is on the core of the body, the exercises we'll be doing to achieve this are consistently helping not just the spine, but all the major organs and systems in the body to attain their optimum function. Again always using the core as its starting point, Yogalates also nurtures healthy functional muscles – imperative for good balance and quality and co-ordination of movement.

The thoracic spine provides a seat of attachment for the shoulder blades via muscle attachments and also the ribcage, which encases and protects the heart and lungs. Once again, the key Yogalates concept of core stability creates correct posture and body alignment, encouraging these major organs to function to their maximum potential.

On to the foundation of our tower, a beautifully curved bone called the sacrum, housed at the back of the pelvis. In Yogalates, we call this the base of the spine. Unique in its composition, the sacrum is made up of five fused vertebrae – and attached to the end of it is the tail bone, called the coccyx, made up of three small bones. The sacrum has the huge responsibility for taking the weight of the whole spine and distributing it evenly through the legs to the ground and from the ground back up to the spine again. The core stability in Yogalates effortlessly maintains the natural curves of the neutral spine and permits the sacrum to do its work of monitoring weight distribution, avoiding stress or strain in any particular area.

'Elongating, lengthening, allowing space for the spine to breathe'

The Structural Tower

Anterior (front) of spine

Cervical spine

'Thoracic Girdle of Strength'

Exit for nerves

Vertebra

Space for spinal disc

Thoracic spine

Lumbar spine

'Abdominal Girdle of Strength'

'Pelvic Girdle of Strength'

Sacrum

Posterior (back) of the spine

Coccyx

It's often said that the pelvic area of the body is the key to good body alignment. But in fact the pelvis and the three divisions of the spine – lumbar, thoracic, and cervical – are all very closely linked and work together in synergy and harmony. The spine channels its direct loading of weight through the sacrum into the pelvis, so if the pelvis is out of kilter – rotated or tilted for instance – the natural curves of the spine can be thrown completely out of balance. A common problem is where one leg is slightly shorter than the other, which in turn causes one shoulder to be lower than the other. But whatever the reason, these kinds of imbalances affect the posture and alignment of the entire body, and trigger knock-on imbalances in the muscular system from head to toe. These are commonly seen as an S- or C-shaped curve (see diagram) when looking at someone from behind, and can cause huge problems, affecting the loading of the spinal column and the function of the central nervous system, and giving rise to all kinds of pain and injuries. Accordingly the pelvis, like the spine, is a vital component in the synergistic functioning of the entire skeleton, and must be correctly balanced and aligned before initiating movement in exercise. And, like the rest of the skeleton, the pelvis takes its part in the Yogalates core principle, ensuring the kind of safe and efficient movement that can achieve fantastic results.

Chapter 4
Yogalates Girdles for Total Toning

Now that we know how important the principle of the core of Yogalates is, it's time to talk about exactly how to maintain strength and balance in that core and make the whole concept really work for us. Imagine our apple core again – the center of the human body. The muscles that lie closest to the core, nearest the skeleton, are the ones which keep the body upright and aligned – and these are the muscles we are targeting in, what's called in Yogalates, the three girdles of strength and synergy. Working and initiating all movement from the three Yogalates girdles, which create core stability, increases the effectiveness of exercise and movement one hundred per cent. All three girdles are anatomically and functionally connected via a kind of internal body stocking – an extensive network of thick connective tissue called the fascia, which knits the muscles of the body together. The fascia is controlled by the activation of muscles and acts as a support to the stabilizing role of the body. The muscles that connect into the fascia of the lower back are the absolute core of core stability, contributing to proper alignment and allowing the three girdles to work in synergy, providing a safe, strong base for any kind of exertion and movement.

The original concept of the Pilates Abdominal girdle of strength led me to investigate the possibility of muscular girdles – not just for the lower back area but for the whole spine. This is when I discovered the Pelvic girdle, and looked further into the concept of scapular (that's the shoulder blades) stabilization. I discovered the intricate connections of the body's fascial system and realized that the Pelvic and Abdominal girdles worked together to create 'core stability'. This made me wonder if the whole concept of scapular stabilization could be developed further to form a third girdle for the upper spine, neck and arms. The idea of three girdles of strength made more sense to me – because that way the whole spine would benefit from muscular support. The result of all this was that I developed the Yogalates Thoracic girdle of strength – meaning that now a muscular girdle existed for each part of the spine. And they are: the Pelvic girdle for the pelvis and legs, the Abdominal girdle for lower back and torso, and the Thoracic girdle for the upper spine, neck and arms. Yogalates exercises target these three girdles, encouraging their synergy with one another, as the unique Yogalates method strengthens and co-ordinates their interplay, further enhancing core stability of the entire spine – and ultimately providing the results we all want.

Now you know just how important it is that when practicing Yogalates you learn to isolate and co-ordinate the girdles, to achieve optimum function and protection during exercise. It may feel strange at first, but using exactly the right muscles will soon become second nature to you and you'll get to know – and love – the often remarked on Yogalates way of 'working and feeling from the inside out'. As we go through the Yogalates exercises in this book you'll learn how to strengthen all three girdles – and once you've started, you won't want to stop. Learning how Yogalates works is all about discovering how true fitness incorporates overall wellbeing and strength of will, as well as physical strength. Only then will you realize your body's potential to be as strong, healthy and beautiful as you've always dreamed it could be. So let's look at the three girdles which are going to help you get that way!

The Pelvic Girdle

This is the foundation of all the girdles. Any kind of movement generates from what I call the pelvic platform and is the base of the Pelvic girdle, which is in turn made up of the group of muscles and ligaments called the pelvic floor. These form a hammock-like sling and run from front to back, attached to the tail bone at one end and the pubic bone at the other, and can be activated by simply imagining that you want to stop going to the toilet – and clenching but not stressing the muscles which do that for you. Like any other area of the body, the pelvic floor, or pelvic diaphragm as it's sometimes known, doesn't function well if it is weak or overstrained. And like any other area of the body, it needs regular exercise. But this is an area largely ignored in mainstream exercise today – a huge mistake, since without a strong pelvic area, no exercise or movement can be of real benefit, and some may even be harmful. Weak pelvic floor muscles are further weakened by the pressure put on them by the upper body during any kind of running, jumping or lifting. This inevitably leads to the unpleasant and uncomfortable problem of involuntary release of urine (known as stress incontinence) and means that the pelvic floor isn't doing its job of supporting the internal organs and keeping them correctly placed.

As well as aiding bladder and bowel function, the Pelvic girdle also houses the reproductive organs and is what we call 'the seat' for sexual sensitivity. Accordingly, it's not hard to work out that a strong healthy Pelvic girdle translates into a good sex life – and the benefits on your relationships don't stop there. This area is also the seat for emotional intuition, meaning that tone and stability in the pelvis enhances the depth and sensitivity of your emotions and feelings, which in turn has a direct effect on the quality of all your interactions with others. On a more scientific note, leading medical researchers back me up in

Yogalates Girdles of Strength and Synergy

saying that the pelvic area is of prime importance when it comes to a strong healthy body and safe effective exercise. Renowned Australian professors of physiotherapy Jull and Richardson (whom I regard as the absolute gurus of core stability) have done masses of research into this subject. Their findings prove beyond any shadow of a doubt that the pelvic floor assists the deep abdominal muscles in creating optimal core stability of the pelvis and lumbar spine, which prevents and also remedies the all too common problem of lower-back pain. Yogalates reflects these findings, and makes them accessible to the general public. So now you can see why I like to give this whole area one hundred per cent focus. A strong and stable Pelvic girdle is an absolute must – not just for whatever kind of exercise or sport you choose to do, but also for smooth, efficient movement in everyday life. Just like a well-constructed building, it's vital to work and build from the inside out to create stability, strength and resilience.

The Abdominal Girdle

The Abdominal girdle works in close synergy with the Pelvic girdle to protect the lower spine and back. It's the base of movement for the lower trunk and works with the diaphragm (breathing muscle) and the pelvic floor muscles to create a cylinder shape of muscles which support the breathing system. If you've ever worn a girdle or a corset of any kind, you'll know the feeling – and look – of being pulled in, up and back to achieve that much-coveted hourglass waistline. But while corsets and their ilk are uncomfortable and bad for your health, creating a natural corset feels – and looks – great. The muscles which do this are called the *Transversus Abdominus*, which wraps around the waist, the *internal and external obliques*, on either side of the waist, and the *multifidus* at the back. Getting this natural corset really working well is great for protecting the internal organs and keeping them nicely in place. And it's also scientifically proven by physiotherapists, that strong *multifidus* muscles, which are attached to the lower spine, are absolutely key to core stability. (See pages 24, 25).

   The Abdominal girdle is activated by drawing the navel back towards the spine, and it's from this center point that each and every movement is initiated, creating a platform for safe effective movement and exercise – and ultimately, a great shape.

The Thoracic Girdle

The Thoracic girdle is the foundation for movement in the upper body, giving our arms power and allowing them range of movement. Its framework is made up of the cervical and thoracic spine and the shoulder blades (scapulae), but its stability comes from the muscles in the center of the

The Musculoskeletal Fusion
The anterior/front of the body

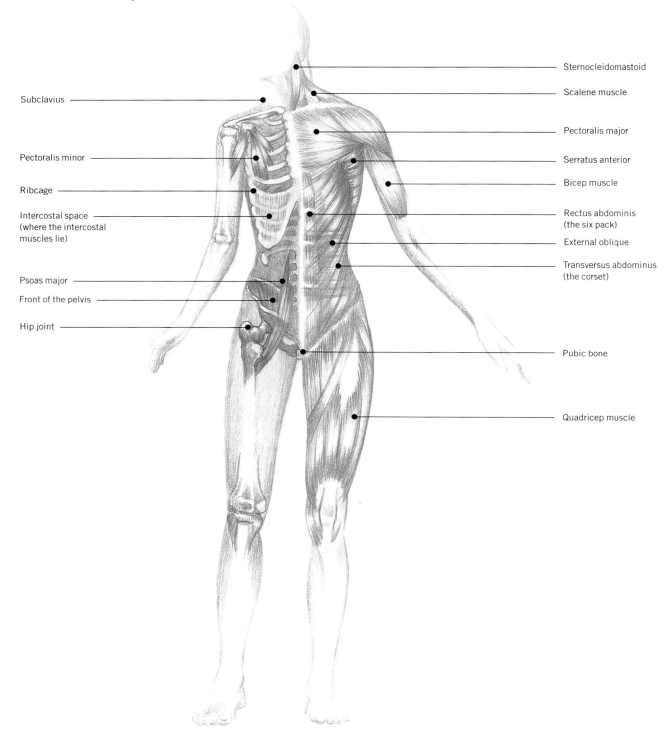

Sternocleidomastoid

Scalene muscle

Subclavius

Pectoralis major

Serratus anterior

Pectoralis minor

Bicep muscle

Ribcage

Rectus abdominis
(the six pack)

Intercostal space
(where the intercostal
muscles lie)

External oblique

Transversus abdominus
(the corset)

Psoas major

Front of the pelvis

Hip joint

Pubic bone

Quadricep muscle

The Musculoskeletal Fusion
The posterior/back of the body

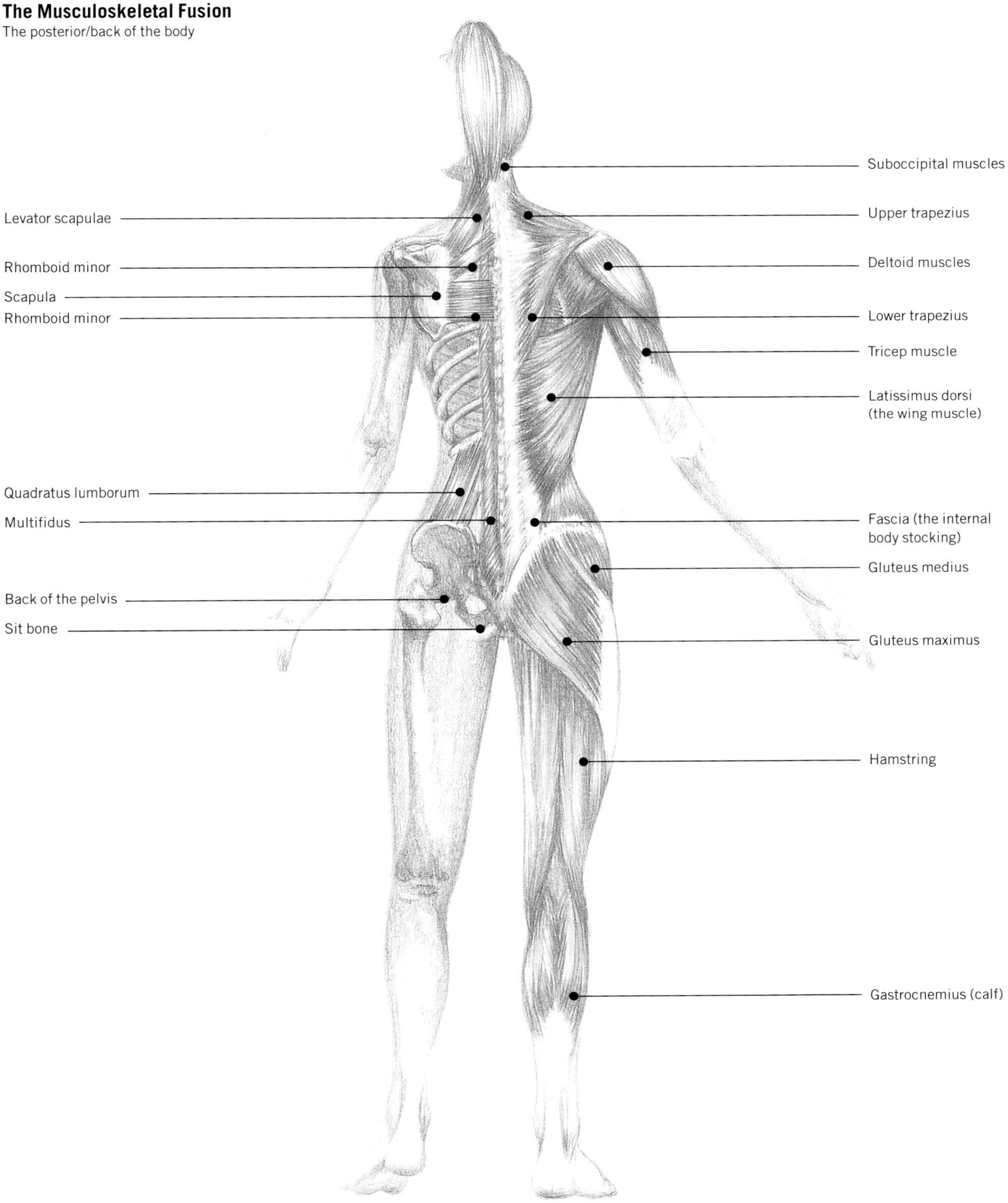

Levator scapulae

Rhomboid minor

Scapula

Rhomboid minor

Quadratus lumborum

Multifidus

Back of the pelvis

Sit bone

Suboccipital muscles

Upper trapezius

Deltoid muscles

Lower trapezius

Tricep muscle

Latissimus dorsi
(the wing muscle)

Fascia (the internal
body stocking)

Gluteus medius

Gluteus maximus

Hamstring

Gastrocnemius (calf)

back and across the chest, as in the pictures on pages 24, 25. These are called the *lower trapezius*, *rhomboids* and *levator scapulae* at the back, and the *pectoralis minor*, *serratus anterior* and *subclavius*, at the front. The *latissimus dorsi*, fanning out on both sides of the back, is also an important player in this area, and when strong, provides much-needed support to these stabilizing muscles. The main function of this group of muscles is to stabilize the shoulder blades during movement, enabling them to slide gently down without rounding forwards or squeezing them together towards the spine.

The shoulders have a great deal of mobility. They can move upwards, downwards, inwards, outwards and they can rotate. This is undoubtedly very useful, but as many of us know to our cost, it also makes the shoulders prone to injury. So it's very important for the muscles in this area to be strong and active – especially in the mid-back, in order to stabilize and create a solid and dependable platform for safe and effective movement. Learning and using the correct placement for the shoulder blades during each exercise is the key to the Thoracic girdle. The shoulder blades should start off close to the ribcage and glide across it, without jerking away, so supporting the Thoracic girdle and creating length in the neck. This is a very important aspect in Yogalates as the length in the neck activates the deep stabilizers called sub-occipitals. These muscles stabilize the head on the tip of the spine and work in conjunction with the mid-back stabilizers to support the 4kg(8-pound) weight of the human head and maintain balance and upright posture. What they'll also do for you is prevent injury and establish the kind of controlled, strong movement which strengthens, elongates and tones, helping you to feel and look the best you possibly can.

Where the *Bandhas* Come In

The word *bandha* is a Sanskrit term meaning to tie or bind together. In Yoga the word refers to postures where certain organs or parts of the body are gripped, contracted and controlled. To describe this in an anatomical and functional way, it is when opposing muscles around any of the joints in the body are simultaneously contracted – creating a wonderful stability for the joint. Using the fascial connections (remember our body stocking), the *bandhas* work together to create forces which push and pull blood and energy throughout the body – contributing to its health and wellbeing. Although historically the *bandhas* are the very essence of Yoga and its *asanas* or postures, in my early days of Yoga practice, I found them to be rarely taught. Or, worse still, taught with very little awareness of anatomical position and function. This was what led to my injury – and my subsequent discovery of the importance of core stability. I realized how the *bandhas* and the girdles of strength could fuse together, and the result was the birth of Yogalates – a safe and effective form of exercise to bring peace to the mind and tone to the body.

Now I'd like us to look at and understand the direct fusion of the three main *bandhas* with the girdles of strength and their functions. One relates directly to the other – they cannot be separated and the three must work in synergy. But the girdles teach us how to isolate each *bandha* and intensify its function for maximum benefit. Because Yoga is so much a part of Yogalates, it's important that you understand its influences. But don't worry about the long names of the *bandhas* – just think of our Yogalates girdles as their Western equivalent. That way when we come across them during the exercises, you'll immediately recognize their function and importance.

So we have *Jalandhara*, sometimes called the throat lock, where the chest is lifted and the chin tucked into the throat with a straight spine. This *bandha* clears the nasal passages and regulates the flow of blood to the heart, head and endocrine glands in the neck – which all translates into feeling and looking healthier! In Yogalates, however, we use a passive or modified version, where the chin is only slightly tucked, creating a lovely extension through the crown of the head and gently elongating the spine. Simultaneously, the shoulder blades are drawn down towards the lower back, which creates stability and protection for the neck and mid-back. The chest naturally lifts, supporting the correct placement of the internal organs and the digestive system. This creates length in the digestive tract and waist, toning the abdominal muscles and aiding core stability at the front of the spine. This is the Yogalates Thoracic girdle of strength.

Uddiyana refers to the part of the body between the diaphragm and the pubic bone, and the *Uddiyana bandha* is the grip exerted when the abdomen is pulled backwards and upwards towards the spine, supporting the internal organs and giving us a streamlined shape. Using our Yogalates breathing system makes this *bandha* work in perfect synergy with the pelvic floor muscles, and has the effect of enhancing the circulation to the internal organs. Each contraction of the abdomen draws a fresh supply of nutrients into each organ, while flushing out toxins – like a sponge. This *bandha* correlates directly to the Yogalates Abdominal girdle of strength.

Mula is a Sanskrit word for root or origin, and in Yogalates it refers to the area where the pelvic and abdominal cavities merge. The *Mula bandha* pulls up the pelvic floor muscles, and the support of this lift enhances the *Uddiyana bandha* – which ties in with the Yogalates Abdominal girdle of strength. But although the lower abdominal contraction is held and maintained with the pelvic platform, the upper abdominal muscles are released, but controlled, allowing the breathing system (discussed in detail in Chapter 6) to move the diaphragm, expanding the lungs. *Mula bandha* massages and tones the reproductive organs, helps the elimination process, nurtures emotional intuition and soothes the nervous system. In Yogic terms, this draws energy in and up through the spine, working in conjunction with the *Uddiyana bandha*, creating an internal heat which aids the digestive system.

Chapter 5

Body Alignment for Beauty and Health

You only have to look around you to see that the human body comes in a huge variety of shapes and sizes. But the posture we should all be striving for – the one that helps us move and exercise safely and effectively – is known anatomically as the Plumb line. As shown in picture 1 over the page, this is where the pelvis and spine maintain their natural – and what should be effortless – curve. In Yogalates we call this the neutral spinal concept, meaning that when you lie down in a relaxed position along the floor with feet, knees and hips in line, there are three natural curves of the spine. This means that the back naturally curves away from the ground in two places – at the lumbar spine, just above the buttocks, and the cervical spine, where the neck begins.

When you stand upright and move around in everyday life you maintain and move in and out of these natural curves, and when you are exercising you need to be aware of them – and make a definite effort to protect them. When you are exercising while lying on your back with both feet off the floor you need to move out of this natural alignment and imprint more of the lower back into the floor for extra protection. Doing this will create a happy spine and a stable pelvis, and when you have the Plumb line posture, the Yogalates girdles will really function to their optimum – simply because this is the position which naturally recruits the correct muscles for any movement, with the minimum of effort. The Plumb line position automatically achieves a balance between the deep core postural muscles and the larger surface muscles, called prime movers, which are responsible for large movements. This keeps the two working together in harmony and, as we've already learned, balance is crucial when it comes to moving and working in a way which keeps the body free of injury and gets the best possible results.

So what happens if the body isn't in the Plumb line posture? When there is a structural imbalance, moving the body away from its natural and correct position, those deep stabilizing core muscles grow weaker, forcing the prime movers to take on their job as well as their own. The result is the development of stress and tension, making these muscles very vulnerable to pain and injury.

Let's look at two very common structural imbalances. First, the Flat Back Type as seen in picture 2 on page 30. Here the natural curve of the lumbar (lower) spine is flattened, possibly through exercising incorrectly. The muscles running down the front of the body, which we often call the six pack

(the *Rectus Abdominus*), pull the shoulders forward towards the hips, further flattening the natural lumbar curve, and often inhibiting upper limb and also lung function. The flattening is made worse by the tightening of the buttock muscles and the hamstring muscles running down the back of the thighs, and all or some of these imbalances have the effect of tucking the pelvis under, putting pressure and strain on the front of the spine.

Going to the other extreme, we have the Sway Back Type (see in picture 3 below). Here the curve of the lumbar spine is exaggerated, caused by tightness in the *Posas* muscles (hip flexor) which connect to the lower spine, passing through the front of the pelvis to the muscles at the front of the thighs (the quadriceps). A similar tightness in the back muscles (the *Quadratus Lumborum* muscles) pulls the back of the pelvis up towards the base of the ribcage – tilting the entire pelvis forward, and putting pressure on

Plumb Line Alignment **Flat Back Type** **Sway Back Type**

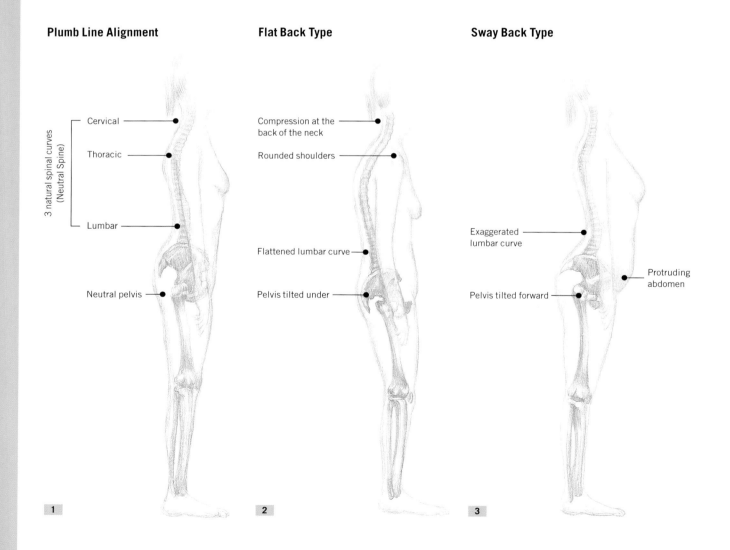

Plumb Line Alignment:
- Cervical
- Thoracic
- Lumbar
- 3 natural spinal curves (Neutral Spine)
- Neutral pelvis

Flat Back Type:
- Compression at the back of the neck
- Rounded shoulders
- Flattened lumbar curve
- Pelvis tilted under

Sway Back Type:
- Exaggerated lumbar curve
- Protruding abdomen
- Pelvis tilted forward

1   2   3

the back of the spine. The end result is a protruding stomach, making it very difficult indeed to pull the navel in towards the spine – and leaving the lower back weakened and unprotected. To check your individual body type you can either use a mirror or ask a friend to take a photo of you. A line drawn down the body will show you which posture your body most resembles. If you are unsure, you can have your body type assessed by a physiotherapist.

So you can see how important the concept of the neutral spine is and how vital it is for your body to be correctly aligned. Not only does incorrect body alignment cause damage, it means that any exercise you do won't have the toning, firming and lengthening effects we all desire. Basic body alignment is one more key Yogalates concept – and another important step along the road to getting the body you've always wanted.

Spinal Alignment

Now that we know how important it is to maintain correct spinal alignment during exercise, let's find out how to put it into practice.

First we'll look at lying long. Just lie down on your back on the floor, legs and feet relaxed and arms by the side of the body, palms facing upwards. Fan your arms out at a 45-degree angle from your body, broadening the mid-back and opening the chest. Just check that your body is in a nice straight line and that the hipbones lie parallel to each other. Now check the neck. If the chin is pointing towards the ceiling, the back of the neck is shortened, leaving it vulnerable to injury. So try and gently bring the chin down so that it's tucked in to the throat (see picture 1). If this is difficult, put a hand towel or two under your head and this will bring your neck into line with the rest of your spine (see picture 2). And if you feel any discomfort in the lower back, put two cushions under the knees. At this point I like to center myself and get in touch with my spinal alignment by using this visualization.

Imagine that you're lying in warm soft sand. Become aware of the breath entering the body and leaving the body, and each time you exhale, sense the body sinking deeper into the sand, imprinting its shape. Now draw your attention to the back of the pelvis where the buttocks meet the base of the spine. Feel the weight of the pelvis anchoring and imprinting its shape connecting the upper body with the lower body.

From the pelvis, visually walk up the spine to the lower back or lumbar spine, which arches naturally off the floor, suspended like a bridge. There's no direct weight or pressure here. Continuing up the spine, the mid-back or thoracic area dives into the floor, curving the opposite way to the lower back. The weight of the mid-back and shoulder blades are broadening, anchoring and imprinting into the floor. Now at this point, I'd like you just to inhale, and hunch the shoulders up, sensing the neck muscles shortening, and the shoulder blades sliding up the spine. Now exhale, and slide the shoulders and the shoulder blades down, away from the ears, down towards the lower back, creating length and integrity in the neck, and allowing it to breathe and relax. This also activates the foundation for the Thoracic girdle of strength, creating another beautifully stable base from which to exert movement – and in Yogalates we are aware of and maintain this position of the neck throughout every practice.

Continuing our visual walk up the spine we come to the cervical spine, or the neck. Like the lumbar spine, it arches gently off the floor, so there is no direct weight or pressure here. Finally we come to the base of the skull, the head, which sits heavy on the floor. These are the three natural curves of the spine, lumbar, thoracic and cervical, which we refer to as our neutral spinal alignment. This is the position that your body likes best, and although we move in and out of this alignment during Yogalates practice, we are always aware of where our neutral spine lies. So take the time now to sense just how your body feels in its natural alignment.

Now we're going to experience the supine rest position. Again, lying long on the floor, place the palms onto the hipbones, fingers towards the pubic

1

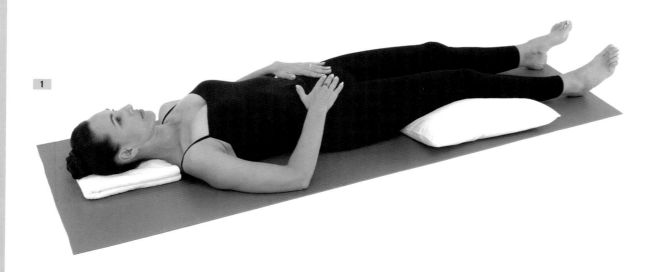

bones (see picture 1). Inhale, and as you exhale, sense the navel sinking towards the spine, and slide the right foot up, keeping it on the floor and bending the right knee. You can feel now that the right hip has sunk towards the floor and that the left hip sits slightly higher. Repeat with the left leg, so that both knees are bent, feet, knees and hips in line, with the feet about 1.5–2 ft (45–60 cm) away from the buttocks. Find a point of balance here – there should be no effort involved (see picture 2). As you move into the supine rest position from lying long, the lower back should flatten slightly, towards the floor – but it still maintains its natural curve, with no direct weight on the lower back.

If your back lifts higher off the floor, you may need to lengthen the lower back by pushing through the heels, lifting the buttocks and tucking the pelvis under. Remember though that when you are in a supine rest position the hipbones should always lie lower than the pubic bone.

Supine rest position places the spine into an anti-gravity position that means that the muscles of the spine and body don't have to work to maintain the position, and there's no pressure on joints, spinal discs, muscles or nerves. So it's very restful for the spine and very safe. This position also helps to elongate the spine, allowing fresh nutrients to reach it and flushing out any toxins. This is a lovely pose and excellent for a tired spine. You can rest and rejuvenate in the supine rest position for ten to twenty minutes every day, breathing slowly and smoothly, just feeling the movement of the breath rippling through the body.

It's from this position that we start to co-ordinate and initiate movement with the breath and commence the lateral thoracic breathing system.

2

Chapter 6
The Breathing System

Breathing through the nose filters and moistens the air, helping the oxygen to enrich the blood and body tissue, and breathing in this way also has the effect of getting the mind to really connect with the body. So during a Yogalates practice we always breathe in and out through the nose – and we use what's called the lateral thoracic breathing system. This teaches you how to engage all three girdles of the body, laying the foundations for keeping you safe while you exercise your way to a better body.

Lateral thoracic breathing means that you try to keep the breath out of the belly and up into the ribcage, expanding the lungs out to the side and stretching the muscles which run in between the ribs, known as the intercostal muscles. This makes the ribcage fan out and expand – not so far as to strain or force the lungs, but just as nature intended. The breath is directed up into the lungs by drawing the navel back in towards the spine and pulling up on the pelvic floor – in the same way that a piston works in a cylinder – to make sure the spine and pelvis are protected during the workout. Even better, doing this has the effect of strengthening the lower back muscles, protecting and massaging the internal organs and toning the abdominals – simply while we breathe. When we inhale, the upper abdominals naturally release a little, to allow room for the diaphragm and the lungs to expand – but we still maintain activation of the lower Abdominal and Pelvic girdles.

'Before any real benefit can be derived from physical exercises, one must first learn how to breathe properly. Our very life depends on it' JOSEPH PILATES

We're fast approaching the section where you're going to get started on the Yogalates exercise program, and we're going to be using the lateral thoracic breathing throughout our Yogalates workout. So let's try it now. To begin the lateral thoracic breathing we first need to observe the natural breath. This is most easily felt in the supine rest position. So, lying on the floor, knees bent, hips, knees and feet in line, find your neutral spine and your neutral pelvis, making sure you're quite comfortable, and let's begin. If you place one hand on your lower abdominal, below the navel, and splay the other hand out to the side on the base of the ribcage, you can feel how your breath moves naturally through the body. Try to create a smooth, even uninterrupted inhale and a smooth, even uninterrupted exhale, just being aware of the breathing and feeling any tension ebbing away.

Notice how, as you inhale, the ribcage and, abdomen rise a little and as you exhale, the ribcage and the abdomen sink softly. To really observe this, take a few deeper breaths, and feel how, as you exhale, the breastbone and the ribcage move away from you towards the pelvis. Also notice how the navel sinks naturally towards the spine, so that you feel weight in this area. The abdominal muscles are naturally sinking and contracting to help you push the breath out of the belly, out of the body. As you inhale again, the muscles release. On your next exhale, just put a little bit more weight into the abdominal area and then, as you inhale, let the weight quickly lift and spring back. Do this a couple of times, experimenting with the feeling of weight in the abdominal area. Then, as you exhale, contract the abdominal muscles and draw the navel back towards the spine. (I like to visualize the abdominals wrapping down around the spine.)

Now, on your next inhale, keep the navel pulled back to the spine. The breath will jump up into the ribcage – and you're doing the lateral thoracic breathing system. Exhale, drawing the navel down and back, and feel the ribcage compress, working alongside the abdominals, creating a flat tabletop as the breath is pushed out of the body. Explore this a few more times by placing both hands on the ribcage, fingertips touching (see picture 1).

Feel the fingertips separate as you inhale and the breath fills the lungs and expands the ribcage out to the sides (see picture 2). As you inhale, the fingertips come back together as the breath leaves the body, breastbone and ribcage pressing down. A great way to really feel this sensation is by lying down and placing a 2kg(4-pound) bag of rice onto the lower abdominals before you start the lateral thoracic breathing system.

Now we'll start to use the breathing system to bring in the pelvic floor muscles, activating the pelvic platform and making the connection between the Abdominal and the Pelvic girdles. Place both hands onto the hipbones, fingers towards the pubic bone, pressing lightly so that you can feel the muscles under your fingertips (see picture 3). On your next exhale draw the navel to the spine, feel the ribcage compressing down, and then pull up on the pelvic floor muscles. Feel the muscles contract and spread right across the front of your pelvis to the hips, as the pelvic platform (otherwise known as the *mula bandha*) activates.

Take some time to explore this breathing system. It will establish your center and is a great preparation for the Yogalates workout you'll be doing.

! **Caution: The lateral thoracic breathing system is not a normal natural breath. It is used specifically in exercising, for the prevention of injury to the pelvis and spine, and should only be used during Yogalates practice.**

→ Never hold your breath. It's worth spending some time to develop a comfortable breathing rhythm.

→ Be careful not to hold any tension in the neck or shoulders when you are using the breathing system.

→ Don't strain the lungs by taking breaths which are too deep, especially if you're a beginner.

→ If you become confused or dizzy at any time when doing the breathing system, stop, return to your natural relaxed breathing rhythm for a few minutes, and then try again.

→ If you experience any pain in the lower back, stop and consult a health professional.

'The breath being the very essence of the body'

Initiating Movement with Breath – The Pelvic Rock

The Pelvic Rock exercise helps to establish what's called a neutral pelvis – which follows the natural curve of the spine, and, as we've learned, is the basis of good spinal alignment. It teaches us to engage the abdominals and then initiate the movement, using both abdominal and pelvic floor muscles to create a connection between the Abdominal and Pelvic girdles and the lumbar spine and pelvis. The Pelvic Rock massages the internal organs and limbers up the lower spine, smoothing the path for mobility between the spine and pelvis – essential for spinal health. This is a great exercise to start off your Yogalates practice since the co-ordination of the breath with the movement creates a flowing rhythm which carries you through the entire workout.

As a general rule we inhale to prepare and exhale on the exertion of movement, unless otherwise instructed. So let's try the Pelvic Rock. Lying down on your mat in the supine rest position, knees bent, feet flat on the floor, place the hands on the hipbones, fingers towards the pubic bone.

1. Inhale to prepare.

2. Exhale, and sense a weight in the abdominal area as the navel sinks towards the spine. Pull up on the pelvic floor muscles, sink the lower back into the floor and feel the pubic bone rise, tucking the pelvis under (see picture 1). This position opens up the back of the spine and closes the front – but don't squeeze the buttocks or grip with the muscles around the front of the hips. All the work should come from the abdominals and the pelvic floor.

3. Inhale and rock the pelvis back past its neutral position, feeling the lower back arch and tilting the pelvis forwards and away from you (see picture 2). This position opens the front of the spine, stretches the abdominal muscles out and compresses the back of the spine.

4. Exhale again and rock the pelvis back to its neutral position (see picture 3). Continue using the breath to move between the two extremes, always being aware of how important it is to link the movement with the breath smoothly and evenly. When you release find your correct neutral spine by sensing the balance between the two extremes.

Moving through this exercise will help bring your hips and pelvis into a state of deep relaxation.

Chapter 7

Principles of Movement

Every minute of our lives we move without even thinking about it. But the quality of our movement greatly affects the result – and as any physiotherapist will tell you, correct and careful movement can save you from serious injury. And during any kind of exercise session or workout, this quality of movement becomes even more important, to protect and guard against damage, and also to give you maximum results – in the form of a body you can be proud of on the beach!

One of the things that makes Yogalates stand out among other exercise systems is its unique principles of movement. Every single time you do a Yogalates workout, you need to build in these principles, from the moment you begin, until the time you finish. They are absolutely crucial for creating a focused, flowing and safe practice and ensuring the kind of correct quality movement that means you'll get great results.

There are six Yogalates principles of movement, all equally important, so let's look at them in turn.

'Creating free-flowing, fluid movements'

Centering with the Breath

The breath is one of the best tools we have with which to create focus and awareness when preparing the mind and body for exercise. When tension is present, either physically or mentally, the body is vulnerable to injury. Using the breath to create a body which is what I call actively relaxed – i.e. the mind is alert but calm and the body is free of any tension – places the body in an optimal state for the recruitment of the correct muscles for movement and activation of the Yogalates girdles.

Drawing the attention to the simple efficiency of the breath as it feeds the body with oxygen and nourishes the cells has a calming effect on the senses and soothes and quietens a busy mind. An ability to let go of thoughts and distractions follows, clearing the head beautifully, and preparing the brain – the control center of the body – to initiate and co-ordinate movement. Sensing the smooth, even, uninterrupted flow of the breath through the inhalation and then the exhalation, naturally disperses all tension, bringing the body to a point of stillness where the only movement is the free-flowing rhythm of the breath. From this point we initiate the Yogalates breathing system and the Yogalates girdles are activated, allowing total control of our movements – and maximum results from our practice.

Alignment

As we've already learned, good body alignment is the key to optimal function of the body, and it's through using this centering phase of our practice that we create the strong mind/body connection which is so important in Yogalates. This in turn leads to an enhanced awareness of correct body alignment and healthy posture of the body, helping us to sense our natural neutral spine and heighten our sensitivity to any individual imbalances and negative tendencies. Once again, this conscious body awareness is carried throughout each and every practice from start to finish. This same awareness means that we can find our neutral spinal alignment in any position – seated, lying or standing – and ensures correct alignment and protection of the spine throughout all movement. Correct placement of the spine and pelvis for each exercise is maintained, enhancing circulation, optimizing muscle function and maximizing that lovely elongation of the spine, allowing it to really breathe.

Neutral Spine

Co-ordination

When we talk about co-ordination we don't just mean co-ordinating movements of the body. Co-ordination of the mind with the body is just as important, so that the two can work in a harmonious way to achieve the physical and mental benefits that regular practice of Yogalates can bring. Part of this is about co-ordinating and synchronising breath and movement, and maintaining it throughout every Yogalates workout. This is really important, and with regular practice it will come naturally – because linking each exercise with the breath promotes balance and co-ordination, building upon the Yogalates principles and resulting in a wonderfully effective sequence of movement. Isolating and co-ordinating the girdles to work in synergy creates a strong center around which each movement revolves. Focusing and concentrating on this ensures the prime quality of each and every Yogalates exercise, avoiding mindless repetition which can lead to bad habits and ultimately be damaging to the body. Remember, Yogalates is more than just an exercise system. It's a perfectly co-ordinated method of moving, breathing and centering, which will change your life.

Strengthening and Stretching

We know that each Yogalates exercise is initiated from a neutral spine – and this alignment ensures that a balance of muscle action is achieved around each and every joint and in and out of every movement. Muscles can only pull on bones and joints – they can't push. So all muscles work in pairs, and when one muscle is contracting around a joint, its opposite number is stretching. In order to maintain a perfect balance, it's important that the muscles are strong enough to hold the joints in a stable position – and also long enough to allow them to travel through their full range of movement. The fascia also plays a big part in this, through its connection to the muscles. The health and smooth functioning of the entire body relies on the interplay of strong flexible muscles, the fascial connections and also the connections to the brain. These, of course, are handled via the central nervous system, which creates a focus and connection with the muscles for that all-important function of the feedback system from the brain to the body.

So you can see now how important it is that any exercise strengthens the muscles that we stretch – and stretches the muscles that we strengthen. Mainstream exercise often loses sight of this vital balance between stretching and strengthening. In Yogalates, however, we take the burden off over-used muscles and gently increase the load on those which are under-used, focusing on attaining a perfect balance of these vital components of physical fitness and wellbeing.

Endurance

Throughout the practice of Yogalates we are constantly building endurance in the musculo-skeletal machine which is the foundation of the body, in order to enhance stamina of both mind and body. As we've already learned, Yogalates gives particular attention to the pelvic floor for its all-important role in core stability – providing the base, strength and stamina needed for safe and effective movement. But building endurance within the muscles is also vitally important, to prevent muscle fatigue and encourage all the body's systems to function as well as they possibly can.

Increased levels of stamina boost the body's natural defences against injury and illness and improve the health of the heart and lungs (called cardiovascular health) as well as general fitness levels.

I like to complement my regular Yogalates practice with an aerobic activity to further boost my cardiovascular fitness. Any exercise that gets you slightly out of breath is ideal – walking, running or cycling, for instance. Personally I prefer to take my aerobic activity outdoors, so that I can benefit from the fresh air at the same time. Walking in the mountains or along a beach is my favourite, where the beauty of nature feeds my soul as well as my body. But it's important to remember to build up your endurance slowly – and never to push yourself. That way you'll guard against injury, and the results that you'll achieve in the end will be long-lasting – and well worth your patience and effort.

Working with the Resistance Band

Relaxation

Taking the time to relax for a period of time at the end of a workout is just as important as all the hard work you've put in. Learning how to really relax your muscles is as crucial to your health and fitness as learning how to contract them properly. Letting your body completely relax and let go allows the body to absorb all the effort you have just put in, and ensures that all the systems and functions of the body come slowly and gently back into a neutral state. There should be no forced contraction of the abdominal or pelvic muscles – the belly should be completely soft, like jelly. In a gentle healing, the physical and mental benefits of our Yogalates workout embrace both mind and body during this relaxation phase, continuing to streamline and lengthen the body, and calming and soothing the nervous system. The body is completely relaxed, the mind is clear and calm and there is a feeling of peace, sensing the breath as it comes into the body, and sensing the breath as it leaves the body.

'Relaxation begins from the outer layer of the body and penetrates the deep layers of our existence' BKS IYENGAR

Chapter 8
Getting Started

Now it's up to you! This is where it all begins. You've learned all the essential things you need to know to get the most out of our practice, and it's time to get started!

First things first. You need plenty of room to move around, and have your equipment close at hand. But before we start, let's take a few moments to recap on what we've learned. It's vital that throughout the exercises, you draw the navel to the spine and pull up on the pelvic floor muscles to activate the Abdominal and Pelvic girdles, and their connection at the pelvic platform. This ensures that the spine and pelvis are protected during movement. I'll be referring to this activation of muscles simply as 'navel to spine'. Always lengthen away from your center, visualizing the shoulder blades drawing down towards the lower spine, elongating through the crown of the head and away through the tail bone, sensing that opposite pull of direction through the spine.

It's equally important to find a soft point of focus with the eyes, a gaze. This helps to quieten the mind and keep it focused internally, in the present moment. This soft point of focus is termed a *Drishti* in Sanskrit – a single line of focus. Sometimes we focus on a part of the body for this – or just focus on a point at eye level. This will be instructed and directed throughout the practice.

Be aware of your fitness level. If you are a beginner, please stay with the beginner's level to start with. This will help to assess your progress, and you can, of course, advance as you feel ready. Remember always to keep the facial muscles relaxed and the jaw soft. This ensures there is no undue tension as you work.

'Physical fitness can neither be achieved by wishful thinking nor outright purchase' JOSEPH PILATES

When training the body, it's really important to create a routine. Both body and mind crave and respond well to regularity. So choose a specific time and place for your regular Yogalates practice and discipline yourself to stick to it. By doing this you'll empower yourself in a way which builds volition, will, determination and focus – underscoring your commitment to your own personal new era of fitness. But remember, too, that the body is in a constant state of change. Energy levels fluctuate from day to day and even from hour to hour. It's vital for the success of your practice that you realize and respect this – and don't always expect to approach your workout with a fresh mind and body. By listening to your body, you'll soon learn to cater to your body's needs and to adjust your workout accordingly. Your Yogalates practice can be used as a tool to manage your energy and feed your body – nurturing and soothing when you need calming, and invigorating and stimulating if you're feeling sluggish. This kind of self-awareness is truly the key to developing a strong and centered body.

Also remember that the time you take to practice Yogalates is your personal time. It shouldn't be a chore, and it definitely shouldn't be competitive – with yourself or with others. So try to develop a practice in which you are focused, aware and present. Simply immerse yourself in each exercise – and enjoy!

Exercising Tips and Cautions:

→ It is vital when exercising that you listen to your body.

→ Do not exercise if you are in pain.

→ If you are taking medication, recovering from injury or surgery, or you are unsure about doing any of the exercises in this program, consult your doctor before you start.

→ Drink plenty of water for general hydration.

→ Do not exercise within two hours of eating a heavy meal.

→ If you experience low energy, drink a fruit juice or eat some fruit while exercising.

→ Do not exercise in a draughty or very warm room.

→ Wear loose and comfortable clothing. Make sure you limber up and warm the muscles through the Yogalates centering phase before you start to execute stronger movements.

→ If you experience any discomfort or dizziness during the practice, stop doing the exercise and go into Child pose (see page 74) or Savasana (see page 132).

→ If you find any of the exercises or poses too strong, return to the beginner's variation until you feel ready for the stronger poses.

→ This workout is not designed for use during pregnancy. However, it is excellent for postnatal women – from six to ten weeks after giving birth.

→ Eating a sensible diet will ensure you get the most out of exercise.

Equipment Needed:

→ Yoga mat (if not, use a blanket)
→ Cushion
→ 2 flat pillows if needed
→ 2 hand towels
→ Belt strap
→ Yogalates Resistance Band (see page 144 for stockists).

Chapter 9
The Abdominal Connection

The whole concept of the abdominal work is to enhance core stability for the protection of the spine and pelvis, creating a trim waist and flat stomach that we all want. We have seen the importance of maintaining a stable pelvis (foundation) for the rest of the spine. Always remember to initiate and execute all movement from your center.

It is important to limber and warm the neck prior to your workout to ensure safe movement, so we will commence with this during the centering phase. We will also work with the stability of the girdles of strength, learning how to rotate them independently and simultaneously and to work them better, and then applying this to the following program.

It is imperative throughout the exercises that you draw the navel to the spine and pull up on the pelvic floor muscles to activate the Abdominal and Pelvic girdles and their connection at the pelvic platform. This ensures the spine and pelvis are protected during movement. I will refer to this activation of muscles simply as 'navel to spine'. Remember to always keep the facial muscles relaxed and the jaw soft: this ensures there is no undue tension as you work.

'Creating the body you want'

Rotations

Begin lying long, centering with the breath. Simply start to deepen your breath, creating an even rhythm. Sense the stability of your neutral spine and body as it anchors into the floor.

Imagine you have a coloured paint brush on the tip of your nose and you are going to start to paint coloured brush strokes across the ceiling.

1. Inhale to prepare.

2. Exhale and allow the weight of the head to roll to the right.

3. Inhale and drag the weight of the head back up to center. Repeat 5 times each side.

4. Inhale and release back to the center, exploring the neck in a neutral position with no tension in the throat. Maintain the length and protection of the neck throughout your practice.

Variation

1. Inhale to one side and exhale to the other, creating a smooth, even-flowing rhythm.

> Learn to release any tension in the neck each time you exhale.

> Be aware if you notice a difference in the quality of movement from one side to the other.

This exercise mobilizes and warms the neck, preparing it for movement. It also teaches you to exercise the neck while the spine is in a stable neutral position.

'Limbering the neck'

'Integrating the breath with movement'

Neck Stretch

In supine rest position interlace the fingers, placing the hands at the back of the head, supporting the weight of your head in your palms. Rest the elbows wide open. See picture 1.

1. Without moving the neck, inhale and wrap the elbows around the ears, dropping the shoulders to maintain length in the neck and prepare it for movement. See picture 2.

2. Exhale, peel the head up, working the chin into the throat as the breastbone moves away from you. Work until you feel a good stretch. See picture 3.

3. Inhale, release the head back down; exhale open the elbows wide.

4. Repeat 3 times.

Variation

1. On the 4th round, keep the head up, take a small breath in.

2. Exhale, rotate the head to the right, again just to where you feel a good stretch down the side of the neck into the shoulder.

3. Inhale, come back to center.

4. Exhale to the other side.

5. Inhale, come back to center.

6. Exhale, release the head back down, and then release the arms beside the body.

This exercise stretches and warms all the important neck muscles for movement and enhances circulation in this region.

'This is not an abdominal crunch; it is a neck stretch'

Shoulder Lifts

Lying in supine rest position, become aware of your neutral spine and center yourself. Tuck the chin into the throat to lengthen the back of the neck, then relax, holding no tension here.

1. Inhale, raise the arms up into the air in line with the shoulders, palms facing each other. Holding this position for a few breaths allow the weight of the arms to sink into the shoulder girdles and onto the floor. Sense the arms just floating and balancing; there is no effort for them to be there. Make sure your facial muscles are relaxed; your jaw is soft. See picture 1.

2. Inhale, raise the right arm up towards the ceiling, peeling the shoulder blade up off the floor. Try not to twist the body or arch the spine. See picture 2.

3. Exhale and release, sinking back down onto the floor.

4. Repeat 5 times with alternative arms.

5. Inhale, bring both arms up together; feel the mid-back broaden.

6. Exhale and allow both arms to sink back down onto the floor.

7. Repeat 2 times.

Then try this stability exercise:

1. Inhale, raise the right arm up.

2. Exhale, take the shoulder down away from the ear and feel the mid-back stabilizing muscles activate. Sense the difference here between the right and left shoulders. The left is relaxed and not stable; the right is active and stabilized. This is engaging the Thoracic girdle.

3. Repeat alternative sides 2 times.

Primarily this exercise limbers and warms the mid-back and neck muscles crucial for effective movement of the Thoracic girdle.

It also teaches you how to activate and isolate the Thoracic girdle of strength, which is great for releasing tension in the neck and the mid-back muscles. Try and deepen your awareness of movement in the upper spine and around the shoulder blades.

Knee Folds

Starting in the supine rest position, ensure the pelvis is in neutral, place left palm on hip bone, fingers to pubic bone. Extend the right hand down beside the body, activating through the fingers.

1. Inhale to prepare, and sense neutral spine.

2. Exhale, draw the navel to the spine and float the right knee up in line with the hip (See picture below). Try not to grip the front of the hip, but keep it as relaxed as possible while you work, making sure the left hip does not lift. Maintain a neutral pelvis.

3. Take a small breath up into the ribcage.

4. Exhale, engage abdominals and pelvic platform, and float the foot down, landing it softly; again the pelvis does not move.

Then try this, enhancing stability even further:

1. As you become more familiar with this exercise you can start to float the knee down, engaging the buttocks and hamstring of this working leg. This further enhances the role of stability in the pelvis.

2. Repeat 5 times exploring one side then the other.

3. Repeat 3 times on the weaker side.

This exercise is excellent for stabilizing the pelvis.

Bring your attention to the back of the pelvis, aiming to keep it still as you move; any rocking of the pelvis indicates pelvic instability. This exercise is great to do daily, always repeating on the weaker side.

Cushion Squeeze 'Activating all three Bandhas and Girdles'

Start in supine rest position, ensuring the pelvis is in neutral; we do not want to tuck the pelvis under or tilt the pelvis away. Place a cushion between the knees, and slightly pigeon-toe the feet, to broaden the back of the pelvis.

Place both palms on the hipbones, fingers towards the pubic bone.

1. Inhale to prepare.

2. Exhale and sense the breastbone moving away from you as the ribcage compresses down, engaging navel to spine and the pelvic platform. Sense the abdominal muscles spread under the palms as they sink and spread down into the pelvic bowl. All this happens as you gently squeeze the cushion.

3. Inhale, release a little.

4. Exhale, streamline the breath, with the abdominal contraction all the way back to the cushion. See picture 1.

5. Repeat 5 times.

Then try this, enhancing stability even further:

1. Exhale, curl the head up as the breastbone moves away from you and extend through the fingers activating the Thoracic girdle of strength. See picture 2. As you consciously engage all three girdles, streamline the breath all the way back to the cushion.

2. Repeat 5 times.

3. Draw the knees to the chest to release the lower back.

The front and back of the pelvis are strengthened and stabilized with this exercise, creating a deep abdominal connection. The back of the pelvis is also broadened, making it excellent for people with sciatica or sacroiliac joint pain. The inner thighs and abdominals are toned.

It also teaches you how to functionally activate and isolate the three girdles of strength, working them in synergy. You learn to carry this throughout the rest of the workout during every pose you do.

❗ Caution: Keep the work out of the neck and the neck tension free.

'Creating that flat table top'

'With the visual of your abdominals imprinting down and wrapping around your spine'

Wide Knees (Inner-Thigh Stretch)

From supine rest position, draw one knee at a time up into the chest; the knees are wide to broaden the back of the pelvis, releasing the lower back, stretching the inner thighs and opening the hips.

Relax here, having a break from the breathing system, allowing the body just to sink and relax into the floor, directing the breath with the mind's eye to where you feel the stretch. See picture 1.

1. Inhale to prepare.

2. Exhale, navel to spine allow the abdominals to sink down into the pelvic bowl, then gently widen your knees and relax the legs.

Variation

You can rotate the feet around the ankles in wide circular rotations. Limber and warm the ankles then reverse the rotation.

1. Inhale in one direction.

2. Exhale in the other.

This helps to pump the blood back a to the heart, aiding circulation in the lower limbs.

Twist rotation:

1. Inhale to prepare.

2. Exhale, draw the right knee towards you, pushing the left knee away; keep the knees bent and widen then hold for 3 breaths. (See picture 2)

3. Inhale, come back to center and repeat other side.

This pose opens the hips, creating a twist and rotation of the lower back and pelvis.

Seated Pelvic Rock Series

Start sitting up tall, balancing on your sit bones with even pressure between the left and right buttocks to create length in the hips, waist, torso and neck, with extension through the crown and a slight tuck of the chin. The feet are 1.5–2 ft (45–60 cm) away from the buttocks; feet, knees and hips are in line. Think of lengthening through your spine.

Sense the neutral spinal alignment with the three natural curves balanced in symmetry on top of each other and the head balancing in the middle. See picture 1.

1. Initiating the breathing system, inhale to prepare.

2. Exhale, draw navel to spine, tuck the pelvis, creating a crease, and fold across the abdominals and a C-curve in the spine, concentrating on breathing in between the shoulder blades. See picture 2.

3. Inhale and spring back up to neutral. Repeat 3 times.

Variation

Hold in the tuck position for 5 breaths.

1. Each time you exhale, scoop the abdominals deeper towards the spine, with the focus of breathing and broadening the mid-back muscles. Sense this expansion in the back of the ribcage and breath into it. See picture 2.

2. Inhale, spring back to neutral, and push past neutral, tilting the pelvis away from you, arching the spine and presenting the chest. Hold it here, sensing the expansion in the front of the ribcage, and breath into it, opening your lungs. See picture 3.

3. Exhale and release back to neutral.

This pose mobilizes and rejuvenates the spine, creating a lumbar pelvic relationship, toning the abdominals and increasing the lung volume.

'Find a point to focus with a soft gaze directly out in front at eye level'

Oblique Curl-Up

Starting in supine rest position, ensuring the pelvis is in neutral, have one hand under the head, the other extended beside the body.

1. Simply inhale and hunch the shoulders up around the ears.

2. Exhale, draw them down activating the Thoracic girdle. This is imperative for the protection of the neck during this exercise.

3. Inhale, lift the elbow of the arm behind your head and drop the shoulder, preparing the neck for movement.

4. Exhale, sense the breastbone moving away from you as the ribcage compresses down, engaging navel to spine and the pelvic platform. Then lift the head to hover 2 inches (5 cm) off the floor, and sense the weight of the head in the hands. See picture 1.

5. Inhale with a small breath up into the ribcage.

6. Exhale, curl the head up, while twisting the upper body, working the shoulder to the opposite knee, getting a sense of ironing the ribcage flat with the abdominals as you crunch to the side. See picture 2.

7. Inhale, release back to a hover and exhale. Repeat 10 times.

The oblique (side) abdominal muscles get a real workout during this exercise, creating the classic hourglass shape.

The rectus abdominis (known as the six-pack muscle) also gets toned while working with the deeper abdominals, enhancing core stability.

❗ Caution: Keep tension out of the throat and the front of the neck by sensing the weight of the head in the hands. The mid-back and abdominal muscles are responsible for supporting the head.

Sense the weight of the head in the hand

1

Use the abdominals to lift the head

Keep the neck long and the throat open

2

Press opposite hip into the floor to keep pelvis neutral

Extend through fingers

Abdominal Roll Down Series

Balancing on your sit bones, this time the feet and knees are pressed together, activating the inner thighs for extra stability.

Holding your hand towel, slide your shoulders down into the mid-back with the Thoracic girdle active and the neck long, lengthening through the spine. See picture 1.

1. Inhale to prepare.

2. Exhale, draw navel to spine, tucking the pelvis under, start to roll down through the spine, with abdominal control, articulating each vertebra into the floor as if you are laying down a string of pearls. See picture 2.

3. As the head touches the floor, inhale the arms up in line with the shoulders. See picture 3.

4. Exhale, bring arms over the head in line with the ears and sense the ribcage compressing towards the pelvis with an opposite pull of direction. See picture 4.

5. Inhale, bring arms back up in line with shoulders.

6. Exhale, start to peel the head and the spine vertebra by vertebra up off the floor (see picture 5). Extend the legs, coming straight into a mid-back stretch.

7. Hold it here for 3 breaths, while you hollow and scoop the abdominals back to the spine and get a sense of separating the lower back from the upper back bending from the waist not the hips. See picture 6.

This exercise really tones the abdominals while mobilizing the spine and strengthening and stretching the back of the whole body. (It teaches you to move through the spine, vertebra by vertebra, allowing the spine to breathe.)

1

2

3

'Balance, co-ordination, moving from a strong center creating free-flowing movements'

'Hollow and scoop the abdominals back to the spine'

4

5

6

Knees to Chest

From supine rest position, draw one knee at a time up into the chest, hugging the knees.

Imagine you have a coloured paint brush in-between your knees and you are going to start to paint coloured circles onto the ceiling. Circle them in one direction then start to explore it and take them wider, really enhancing the massage on the lower back and pelvis.

Create a smooth even breath with a smooth even circle 5 times and then reverse rotation.

This pose broadens and massages the lower back and pelvis, releasing tension, and enhancing co-ordination and circulation.

Full Body Stretch

From the previous pose we extend the legs, lying long, making sure the lower body is in line with the upper body.

1. Inhale, raise arms up into the air.

2. Exhale, bring arms over the head and extend through the fingers and toes, activating the whole body, breathing into the stretch and sensing the whole body active. Lengthen away in opposite directions, extending from your center.

Passive Back Bend

1. From the Full Body Stretch inhale and spring the ribcage up off the floor towards the ceiling, arching the spine. (See picture)

2. Exhale, compress base of ribs to the floor and the abdominals to the spine, but do not compress the lower back into the floor – maintain neutral spine here. Repeat 4 times.

3. Inhale, bring arms back up; exhale and release them beside the body.

This pose stretches the whole front and back of the body, stretching the abdominals and elongating the spine. It opens the chest and the front of the spine while again teaching how to compress the abdominals on the exhale.

Supine Twist

Lying long, placing the right foot onto the left knee, left hand onto the right knee, extend the right arm out in line with the shoulder, palm facing down.

1. Inhale to prepare.

2. Exhale, engage navel to spine and draw the knee across the body to where you feel a comfortable stretch. Extend through the left toes.

3. Tuck the chin to the throat and turn to look over the right hand. Hold this for 5 breaths, and each time you exhale try to take the stretch deeper. See picture.

4. Exhale, engage navel to spine and release back to the center. Repeat other side.

5. Inhale and release into Savasana (see page 132).

This exercise stretches the side abdominals and works the deep spinal rotators aiding stability of the spine at a deep level. The chest and front of the shoulder are stretched and opened. As you release from the twist the internal organs and discs receive a fresh supply of blood and nutrients.

Chapter 10

The Upper Body

These exercises focus on the upper body and arms, and define and strengthen the arm and chest muscles while at the same time strengthening the mid-back and spine. This in turn creates the foundation for that all-important Thoracic girdle of strength, which supports and protects the neck and aids in upper limb movement.

It is imperative throughout the exercises that you draw the navel to the spine and pull up on the pelvic floor muscles to activate the Abdominal and Pelvic girdles and their connection at the pelvic platform. This ensures the spine and pelvis are protected during movement. I will refer to this activation of muscles simply as 'navel to spine'. Remember to always keep the facial muscles relaxed and the jaw soft; this ensures there is no undue tension as you work.

'Physical fitness can neither
be achieved by wishful thinking
nor outright purchase'
JOSEPH PILATES

Virasana (Supported)

Kneel supported by your cushion, place feet in line with the hips, toes pointing directly away from you, and sit back onto your heels.

Take a moment to sense your balance. Sit up tall, place even weight between your left and right sides, creating length in the hips, waist, torso and neck. Extend through the crown of the head and slightly tuck the chin, lengthening through your spine.

You can feel the ribcage balanced over the hips, the shoulder girdle balanced over the ribcage and the head balanced on top. This is your neutral spine.

'Find a point of focus with a soft gaze directly out in front at eye level'

'Sense the breath lengthen and ride the spine then sense it release and soften the spine'

'Balance, poise and lightness'

Shoulder Hunches

Sit in supported Virasana (see opposite), hands resting on the thighs. Maintain neutral spine, and without moving the spine or neck:

1. Inhale, hunch the shoulders up around the ears. See picture 1.

2. Exhale, slide them down and repeat 3 times.

3. Isolate – inhale, hunch the right shoulder up, then the left. See picture 2.

4. Exhale, slide the right shoulder down followed by the left.

5. Repeat leading with the left shoulder.

The mid-back muscles are warmed and limbered in this exercise, preparing them for the activation of the Thoracic girdle. Correct placement of the shoulder blades is learned, allowing the release of tension in the neck and shoulders.

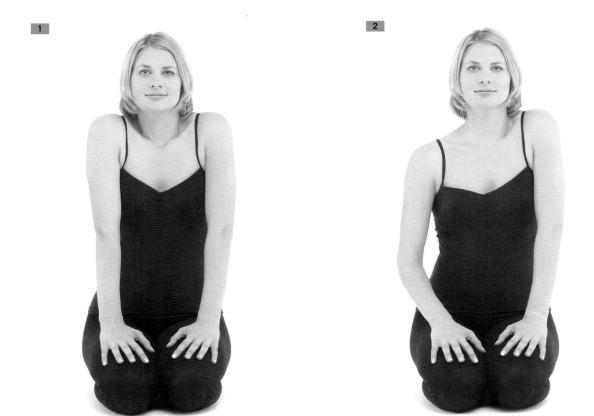

67

Rotate and Isolate

Sit in supported Virasana (see page 66).

1. Inhale and extend the arms out to the side in line with the shoulders, lengthening through the fingers. See picture 3.

2. Exhale and draw the shoulders down away from the ears, activating the mid-back muscles.

3. Inhale, rotate both palms up towards the ceiling, sensing the shoulder blades move down towards the lower back, opening the chest.

4. Exhale, rotate the palms around in the opposite direction – sense the shoulders hunching forwards and up towards the ears. See picture 2.

5. Repeat 5 times.

6. Isolate – keep right palm up and rotate just the left back around. See picture 3.

7. Reverse rotation, alternating one shoulder blade up then one down. Repeat 5 times.

This exercise massages the mid-back muscles and teaches co-ordination between the right and left side of the body. The mid-back muscles receive a massage, making it excellent for anyone who works on computers as it releases tension in the nerves which run from the neck all the way to the fingers. Through this exercise you learn to sense the natural function of the upper limbs as the arms and shoulder blades work together in synergy to produce movement, creating definition in the arms.

1

2

3

Side Push-Up

Sitting with your legs to the side (beginners may sit on cushions), place hands shoulder distance apart onto the floor. Keep the neck long and in line with the upper spine.

Beginners:

1. Inhale to prepare.

2. Exhale, draw navel to spine; bend elbows out to the side taking the face towards the floor. Feel your abdominals grip to support this move. See picture 1.

3. Inhale, push the palms into the floor and back up. Repeat 10 times.

Advanced one-arm push-up:

Start with the legs to the left of the body, left hand to floor, right palm on the chest, taking right ear to the floor.

Turn the body to the front, still maintaining the upper spinal alignment.

1. Inhale to prepare.

2. Exhale, draw navel to spine; bend the elbow to the side taking the ear to the floor. Feel the side upper abdominals working to support you here. See picture 2.

3. Inhale, push back up. Repeat 5–10 times.

This exercise strengthens and tones the tricep muscle at the back of the arm and shoulder cuff.

The entire shoulder girdle is toned and strengthened during this exercise. Particularly targeted are the muscles around the armpit and tricep at the back of the upper arm.

1

2

'The upper-body definer'

'The tricep enhancer'

Mermaid Stretch

Still sitting with legs to side of body:

1. Inhale, raise the outside arm up and drop the shoulder, creating length in neck; other hand to the floor. See picture 1.

2. Exhale, draw navel to spine and bend the body to the side, taking the arm over the head and creating a lateral C-curve. Breathe into the upper lung, flaring the ribcage towards the ceiling, elongating the spine and carving an arch between your body and the floor as you do so. See picture 2.

Variation

1. Inhale, come back to center, take hold of the ankle.

2. Exhale, lift the other arm up and lean over to the other side.

3. Repeat the sequence 5 times.

4. Repeat sequence on other side.

Through stretching the sides of the body, we open the upper ribcage and lung, increasing lung capacity, stamina and circulation. The back is flexed, mobilizing the discs and spine, and opening the joints at the side of the spine, allowing the spine to breathe.

'Creating free-flowing, fluid movements'

'The great outer body stretch'

Advanced One-Arm Balance

Sitting on the left side of your buttocks, place the left hand onto the floor, fingers pointing to the side.

1. Inhale to prepare.

2. Exhale, draw navel to spine; push weight through the palm and extend the right leg. Place the left leg under and behind the right and lift the hips off the floor towards the ceiling. Balance here, stabilizing your body by activating all three girdles. See picture 1.

3. Inhale, bring the top arm up and over; lift the hips away from the floor. Sense an opening through the right side of the body and chest.

4. Tuck your chin into the throat and look to the floor.

5. Hold as long as you can and maintain a smooth breath through the pose. See picture 2.

6. Inhale, release down and repeat on the other side.

This exercise is a total body toner. It activates and strengthens all three girdles, deepening their connection with one another, enhancing core stability. The pose builds endurance and stamina and enhances co-ordination and synergy of the muscles, improving general balance, function and shape.

1

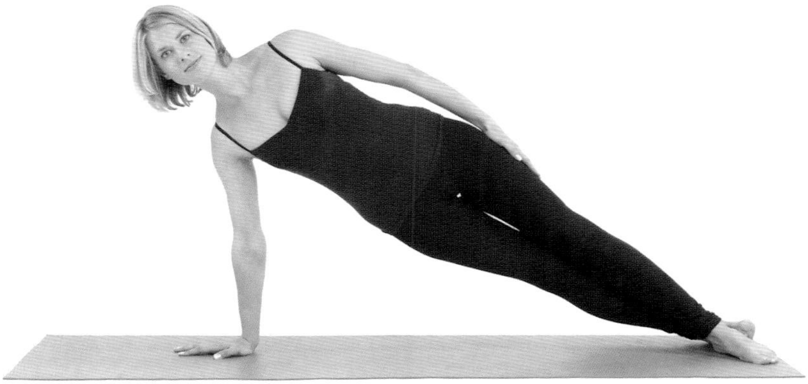

2

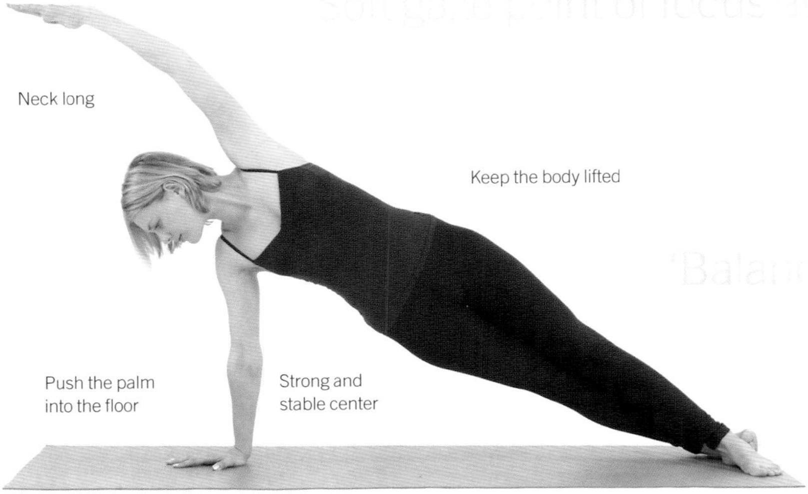

Neck long
Keep the body lifted
Push the palm
into the floor
Strong and
stable center

'Soft gaze point of focus at the fingers'

'Balance, poise and lightness'

Cat (Marjariasana) 'The deep abdominal toner'

Begin on all fours, like a cat. Check your alignment. The wrists are placed in line with the shoulders and the knees in line with the hips; thighs are vertical. The palms are spread evenly onto the floor, with the middle fingers pointing forwards.

Find your neutral spine by extending through the crown of the head and tail bone. Direct the gaze between the hands; the neck is in line with the rest of the spine.

Maintain length in the neck, by activating the Thoracic girdle and sliding the shoulder blades down the mid-back.

! Caution: If you experience any pain in the wrists, you can roll a blanket or towel and place it under the heel of the palms to decrease the angle at the wrists. Use this extra support for any of the Cat variations. If the poses are still too strong, simply rest back into the Child pose (see page 74).

Extend

Do not move the spine

Extend

Contract abdominals up to spine

Abdominal and Pelvic Lift

Without moving the spine:

1. Inhale to prepare.

2. Exhale, draw navel to spine with 5 small contractions, engage the pelvic floor, and sense the abdominals hollow back to the spine. Feel the connection between the Abdominal girdle and the Pelvic girdle.

3. Inhale and release the abdominals toward the floor.

4. Repeat 5 times.

Through toning and strengthening the abdominal and pelvic floor muscles we create more definition in the waist at the same time as building that all-important core stability.

'Soft gaze, with point of focus between the hands'

Extend

Do not move the spine

Extend

Contract abdominals up to spine, then pull up the pelvic floor

Cat and Back Extension

Start in Cat pose. Be sure to check your alignment. Do not sag into your shoulders, but lift upwards out of the shoulders, pushing through the hands.

1. Inhale to prepare.

2. Exhale, draw navel to spine with 5 small contractions; engage the pelvic floor.

3. Inhale – take a small breath into the lungs while still maintaining abdominal and pelvic floor contraction.

4. Exhale, extend the right arm and left leg out from the center, reaching through the fingers and extending through the toes, squeezing the buttocks.

5. Hold for 2 breaths.

6. Inhale and release back to all fours.

7. Repeat 5 times on each side.

! Caution: If you experience any discomfort in the lower back, do not lift the leg so high.

The buttock and arms are toned and the spine is elongated through this extension exercise. More importantly, you build strength in the three girdles as we initiate them to find our balance, improving stability at your core. As your focus and concentration are developed, stamina, equilibrium and harmony of the mind and body are also improved.

'The abdominal extender'

'Lengthen, reach and extend'

73

UPPER BODY FLOW SERIES

Child (Balasana)

Folding the body into the pose of the child, the arms are relaxed by the sides of the body. There is no tension in the neck and shoulders.

This pose is grounding as it rests the bodily systems. It relaxes, restores and cools the body, so is an excellent one to add intermittently throughout your practice to rejuvenate you for the next pose.

To come out of Child pose, draw the navel to the spine and slowly start to curl the body up to sitting, moving the spine back to neutral. Reload the weight of each vertebra on top of vertebra, restacking the ribcage, with the head and shoulders the last to come back up on top.

! Caution: If the forehead doesn't come to the floor, form two fists one on top of the other under the forehead; if you're feeling discomfort in the hips sit back on cushions, and support upper body on forearms or cushions.

Uttanasana

From the pose of the Child, place the hands onto the floor in front of the knees, palms down; turn the toes under, feet in line with the knees and hips.

1. Inhale to prepare.

2. Exhale, draw navel to spine; bring yourself up to standing with the body folded forward. Keep the knees and spine soft, allowing the body to hang over the legs to a level that you are comfortable with and can control. See picture below.

It is important here to keep the navel drawn in, creating room for the body to fold and protecting the lower back at the same time.

! Caution: If you feel any discomfort in your back, curl straight up to standing. If you experience low blood pressure, take caution coming out of this pose.

Tricep Squat

From Uttanasana, keep the head and shoulders folded and knees bent.

1. Inhale to prepare.

2. Exhale, draw navel to spine and slowly roll up, rebuilding the spine, stacking each vertebra on top of the next, coming up to a standing squat. Make sure the knees are in line with the middle toes, arms beside the body.

3. Moving the arms, turn palms to face backwards. Inhale to prepare.

4. Exhale, bring the arms back behind the body. Use a visual image of compressing the air backwards with very active arms. See picture below.

5. Inhale and release the arms to the side of the body, keeping them active.

6. Repeat 10 times.

'Removing the upper arm flab'

'Sensing the ambience within'

Utkatasana

From Tricep Squat:

1. Inhale to prepare.

2. Exhale, extend the arms forward in line with the shoulders, palms facing each other. Extend through the fingers, arms are active.

3. Hold for 5 breaths. See picture below.

4. Try to squat a little deeper with each exhale, still maintaining alignment and watching the knees are positioned above the middle toes.

5. Inhale, release the arms and straighten the knees.

6. Repeat 2 times.

Spinal Roll Downs

From Utkatasana:

1. Inhale, soften the knees and nod the head. See picture 1.

2. Exhale, draw navel to spine, and roll the body back down into Child pose.

3. Rest in Child pose for 8 breaths. See picture 2.

This series is excellent for mobilizing the spine and stretching the back of the body. It strengthens the triceps and mid-back muscles, shoulders, abdominals and upper thighs, building stamina and endurance. Uttanasana is an inversion, it brings fresh blood to the brain, oxygenating and rejuvenating the mind. By having the head lowered and the torso tilted in this way, any stress on the musculature and organs of the torso is reduced, which brings about balance and efficient functioning of all the bodily systems, creating an inner radiance.

75

Shoulder Stretch

Align the body in Cat pose (see page 72).

1. Inhale to prepare.

2. Exhale, draw navel to spine, bend the left elbow to the side and slide the right arm along the floor, resting the right shoulder and the right side of the head on the ground, creating a twist at the waist and a rotation of the spine.

Variation

3. If comfortable here extend the left arm into the air, tuck the chin into the throat and gaze up at the top thumb lifting the shoulder away from the ear.

4. Extend through the fingers to open the chest. Hold for 5 breaths. Work with the visual of breathing up into the top lung, expanding the ribcage to the side.

5. Inhale, release the arm down.

6. Exhale, come back to the Cat.

7. Repeat the other side and then rest into Child pose (see page 74).

Sense whether one side feels tighter than the other and repeat on the tighter side.

Due to the twisting action of this exercise, the shoulders, mid-back muscles and deep rotators of the spine all get a good stretch, making it particularly beneficial for those with scoliosis. Focus is placed on expanding and opening one side of the chest and lungs at a time.

'Keeping facial muscles relaxed and the jaw soft – no tension as you work'

'Upper-body rotator'

Breathe into your top lung

Shoulder down away from ear

Reach through fingers

Chest Stretch 'The neck lengthener'

Sit in supported Virasana (see page 66), and interlace the fingers behind the back.

Beginners:

1. Inhale to prepare.

2. Exhale, draw navel to spine and activate mid-back muscles, squeezing the shoulder blades together. Opening the chest, work the arms up and away from the body. Slightly nod the head forward, sensing the depth of the stretch. See picture 1.

Advanced:

Sit in supported Virasana (see page 66), and interlace the fingers behind the back.

1. Inhale to prepare.

2. Exhale, draw navel to spine and activate the mid-back muscles, squeezing the shoulder blades together. Open the chest and work the arms up and away from the body. Slightly nod the head forwards.

3. Inhale, then exhale navel to spine, coming up onto the knees and carefully placing the forehead onto the floor. Keeping the neck very stable, roll up onto the crown of the head until you feel a stretch down the back of the neck.

4. Inhale, bring arms up and over the head. Hold for 2–3 breaths. See picture 2.

5. Exhale, release arms down and fold into Child pose (see page 74).

This is an excellent pose for opening the chest and stretching the arms and shoulders. The back of the neck is also deeply stretched, helping to release any tension held there.

❗ **Caution: If you have any neck or shoulder pain/injuries, stay at the beginner's level.**

'The chest booster'

1

Squeeze shoulder blades together

2

Extend through arms

Neck long

Navel to spine

Anchor crown of head

Chapter 11

The Lower Body

This chapter focuses on the lower body. These exercises tone the buttocks, building endurance and creating definition in the muscles, while strengthening and sculpting the legs. The lower back and pelvis will also be strengthened, and again the abdominals will be toned, creating core stability.

It is imperative throughout the exercises that you draw the navel to the spine and pull up on the pelvic floor muscles. This activates the Abdominal and Pelvic girdles and strengthens their connection at the pelvic platform, ensuring the spine and pelvis are protected during movement. I will refer to this activation of muscles simply as 'navel to spine'. Remember to keep the facial muscles relaxed and the jaw soft, ensuring there is no tension as you work.

'Sculpting the buttocks'

'The anti-cellulite solution'

Bridge (Setu Bandhasana)

Start in supine rest position (see page 32). Then bring the feet a little closer towards the buttocks. The arms are extended beside the body with active hands and fingers. It is important to activate the Thoracic girdle, drawing the shoulders away from the ears; creating length and protection of the neck.

Commencing with the concept of the Pelvic Rock (see page 39):

1. Inhale to prepare.

2. Exhale, draw navel to spine, sink the lower back and peel the pelvis up off the floor, creating a crease and fold across the abdomen.

3. Inhale, release back to a neutral pelvis. As you release it, massage the lower spine and broaden the back of the pelvis onto the floor.

4. Repeat 3 times. See picture 1.

5. Advancing the work, exhale, peel the pelvis and then just the base of the ribcage off the floor. See picture 2.

6. Inhale, release the spine and imprint each vertebra back into the floor, coming back to neutral. This will intensify the sensation, bringing your awareness to any segments of your spine that feel blocked or stuck together. Taking the focus of the mind there, use the breath and motion to uncoil your spine.

7. Take it a step further. Remove the hand towel. Exhale, draw the navel to the spine, peeling the pelvis, the base of the ribcage, then the mid-back up off the floor, resting on the shoulder blades, in the Bridge. Squeeze the buttocks and sense one line from breastbone to pubic bone; keep the hips lifted and even. See picture 3.

8. Watch that the knees do not roll in or splay out, maintaining even pressure on the feet.

9. Hold for 3 breaths and repeat 5–10 times.

As you mobilize and strengthen the spine, you rejuvenate the spinal discs, cord and nerves, which play such a vital role in our overall body maintenance and function. By moving each of the vertebrae, we bring balance and symmetry to our structural tower.

The buttocks, abdominals and back of the thighs also benefit from this pose.

! Caution: You should feel no tension in, or strain on, the neck. If you do, release back down, and continue just to where you are comfortable.

1

2

3

'Unwind your spine'

One-Legged Bridge Balance (Advanced)

Commence in the Bridge (See opposite).

1. Place the hands up under the lower back and pelvis. If comfortable, balance here for a moment and breathe. See picture 1.

2. Inhale to prepare.

3. Exhaling, engage navel to spine then raise the right leg high in line with the right hip. Point the toes towards the ceiling. See picture 2.

4. Hold and sense your balance.

5. Exhale, navel to spine, flex the foot and lower the leg in line with the left knee; working with control from your abdominals, squeeze your buttocks.

6. Inhale, point the foot.

7. Exhale, engage the abdominals and raise the leg back up. Repeat 5 times.

8. Inhale to release the foot to the floor; exhale, take the other leg up. Repeat as above 5 times. Then inhale, release foot to the floor.

9. Exhale, roll your spine down. Draw the knees into the chest to release the lower back.

This pose is a passive inversion and a strong back bend. It opens the front of the chest and spine, releasing anterior pressure on the spinal discs. It strengthens the whole of the back of the spine, giving the thighs and buttocks an overall tone.

It aids in venous return, reducing fluid retention in the ankles, and delivers a fresh supply of oxygen to the brain. The thyroid glands in the neck are stimulated, helping to regulate the hormonal system and bring balance and harmony to the body.

1

2

'Balance, poise and lightness'

Single Leg Crunch

From supine rest position (see page 32) draw both knees into the chest. Beginners or people with neck problems place a cushion under your head. Place the left hand onto the right knee, right hand onto the right ankle.

1. Inhale to prepare.

2. Exhale, navel to spine, extend the left leg up into the air, pointing the toes (see picture 1). You can either stay in this position or lower the leg towards the floor, coming to a position where you are comfortable – no lower than a 45-degree angle.

3. Inhale and prepare again.

4. Exhale, navel to spine, activate the Thoracic girdle, and draw the shoulders away from the ears. If comfortable with your neck, peel the head up off the floor, coming to a classic crunch position. See picture 2.

5. Inhale and swap legs, taking hold of the left knee and ankle.

6. Exhale, engage abdominals and extend right leg either straight up or to your comfortable position.

7. Repeat 10–20 times.

8. Release, draw both knees into the chest, and rock the body side to side, releasing the lower back.

All of the abdominal muscles including the deep, side and the top layer are toned with this exercise. It strengthens the calf muscles and front of the thighs and teaches co-ordination of the upper, lower, left and right sides of the body. This is a great exercise to shape the waist and flatten the tummy.

1 BEGINNERS

2 ADVANCED

Side-Lying Breathing

Sitting with the legs to the side, line the heels up with the buttocks, and lay yourself down onto your side, extending the lower arm long. Place a folded hand towel in between your ear and lower arm, aligning the upper spine with the lower spine. Place the upper hand onto the top hip and stack the hips on top of each other, aligning the pelvis and lower spine, finding your neutral alignment. Use the visual of suspending the waist up off the floor. Place the hand under the side of the body, cupping the waist in the palm.

1. Inhale, breathe into the hand, allowing the abdominals to expand. See picture 1.

2. Exhale, draw navel to spine and sense the base of the ribcage and the waist lift away from the floor as the ribcage compresses with the abdominals. See picture 2.

3. Inhale, release the abdominals again. Repeat 5 times.

This exercise teaches you to initiate the breathing system in a side-lying position. It tones the waist and abdominals, creating a strong foundation for the exertion of movement in this position.

1

2

Lengthen the neck

Stack the hips

Suspend the waist

TOTAL LEG TONER

The Clam, Single Leg Circles, Inner Thigh Lift and Bicycle exercises can all be linked together for a total leg toner. First work through all four exercises with one leg, then repeat the sequence on the other side.

'Sculpting a shapely figure'

'Total butt toner'

The Clam

Start in the Side-Lying Breathing position (see page 83). Hold your waist up off the floor through the activation of the Abdominal and Pelvic girdles.

Place your upper hand in front of the chest for extra stability if needed.

1. Inhale, hunch the upper shoulder towards the ear, shortening the neck muscles.

2. Exhale, slide the shoulder away from the ear, lengthening the neck; maintain this position.

3. Inhale to prepare.

4. Exhale, navel to spine, maintaining neutral spine. Keep the feet together, open the knee towards the ceiling and squeeze the butt – no movement in the pelvis. See picture below.

5. Inhale, release back down. Repeat 10–20 times each side.

Both the deep and superficial buttock muscles are toned and strengthened, while the inner and outer thighs are firmed in this exercise, helping to stabilize the pelvis and hips.

Side Leg Circles

Start in Side-Lying Breathing position (see page 83), the lower knee bent, the heel in line with the buttocks. Extend the top leg long with the toe softly pointed.

1. Inhale to prepare.

2. Exhale, navel to spine, and begin to draw small circles with the top leg in one direction 10 times, breathing into it. See picture below.

3. Reverse rotation.

Variation

1. If comfortable, take circle wider, keeping pelvis stable, and reverse rotation.

2. Inhale, release the leg back down.

As you circle the upper leg, you limber and strengthen that hip joint, firming the buttocks and the side of the leg, creating definition in them.

Inner-Thigh Lift

Start in the Side-Lying Breathing position (see page 83). This time bend the top leg, taking hold of the ankle, and place the foot onto the floor. If this is uncomfortable, rest the top knee onto your cushion. Extend the bottom leg long and flex the foot. Anchor the shoulders away from the ears.

1. Inhale to prepare.

2. Exhale, navel to spine, pull up on the pelvic floor then lift the lower leg, activating the inner thigh (see picture below). Make sure to engage the abdominals, pelvic floor and inner thighs as these three work together. Do not leave one behind.

3. Inhale, release but do not collapse.

4. Repeat 10–20 times both sides.

This exercise specifically targets the pelvic floor and inner thigh muscles, firming and strengthening the inside of the leg. The side abdominals work strongly to stabilize the body, enhancing the body's corset.

Contract the navel, pelvic floor then the inner thigh to lift the leg

Bicycle

Start in Side Leg Circles position (see page 85).

1. Inhale, draw the knee into the chest.

2. Exhale, draw the navel to spine and extend the leg forwards in line with hip, flex the toes then sweep the leg down keeping it parallel to the floor.

3. Inhale, extend the leg past the hip, behind the body, and point the toes, just like riding a bicycle. See picture 1.

4. Repeat 10 times each side.

Variation
Hold the heel towards the buttocks for 5 breaths, stretching out the front of the thigh. See picture 2.

All of the leg is toned and the hip joint is mobilized as you practice this exercise. This creates stability around the pelvis, promoting co-ordination.

'Creating a free-flowing smooth movement'

Prone Butt Strengthener

Lie on your stomach, making sure you are comfortable (you can lie over your flat pillow if necessary). Place one hand onto the other, then rest the forehead down, maintaining length in the neck, again sensing your neutral spinal position.

Sense for a moment how, in this position, the breath moves through the body. On the inhale the breath elongates and lengthens the spine and on the exhale the spine condenses and compresses, especially felt in the lower back area. Observe this for 5 breaths.

1. Inhale to prepare.

2. Exhale, draw the navel up off the floor engaging the pelvic floor muscles by pushing the pubic bone slightly into the floor. Sense the stability this creates around the pelvis and the lower back.

3. Repeat 5 times to sense how the breathing system functions against gravity in this position.

4. Exhale, draw the heels together, also squeezing the buttocks and legs together, the feet will hover an inch off the floor.

5. Inhale, allow the feet and legs to release and naturally roll outward, pigeon-toeing the feet.

6. Repeat 5–10 times.

Variation

1. On your next exhale, simply lift the legs a little way off the floor, keeping them together and active, kneecaps lifted. The focus is not how high you can lift the legs but how far you can extend and elongate out from the hips.

2. Inhale, release.

3. Repeat 5–10 times.

4. Inhale, release into Virasana (forward) (see page 88).

This pose targets the deep rotators of the hips, which are largely ignored in mainstream exercise. These muscles play an essential role in pelvic stability, aiding balance and co-ordination during walking, running, and all dynamic activities. The muscles of the hips are firmed, while the buttocks are toned, creating definition in the legs.

! Caution: If you experience any lower-back pain do not lift the legs up off the floor until you are strong enough.

Squeeze heels · Squeeze inner thighs · Squeeze buttocks · Navel to spine · Neck long

Virasana (Forward)

Starting in Child pose (see page 74), take the knees apart slightly (this helps to stabilize the body for the lateral stretch).

1. Inhale to prepare.

2. Exhale, extend both arms in front of the body, reaching through the fingers and activating the arms.

3. Hold for 8 breaths and surrender into the pose. See picture 1.

Variation

Add a lateral stretch if desired.

4. Exhale, walk the hands to the right, taking the spine and pelvis with you until you feel a stretch down the left side of your torso. Keep the navel drawing up: this gives the body room to bend while protecting the lower back. See picture 2.

This pose stretches the buttocks, lower and mid-back, the shoulders and arms. It is a rejuvenating resting pose which soothes and calms the nervous system. The lateral variation stretches the muscles that run vertically along the spine, stimulating the kidneys and aiding in detoxification.

1

Breathe into your spine

'Butt stretcher'

2

Wrist Rotations

Start in Supported Virasana
(see page 66).

1. Exhale, extend through the fingers.

2. Inhale, release. Repeat 5 times.

3. Exhale, hold the extension and simply rotate the hands around the wrists 10 times, then reverse rotation opening the front and back of the wrist.

4. Inhale, keep breathing, relax and shake the hands out.

'Rotating and limbering'

'Keep a soft gaze, and a point of focus'

Wrist Stretch

This is a variation of the Wrist Rotations. Extend the arms straight out in front in line with the shoulders.

1. This time simply inhale, and exhale, flex the wrist by pulling the fingers towards you 'pushing through the palm' and hold for 3 breaths. See picture 1.

2. Inhale, release the hand forwards, fingers now pointing to the floor, opening the front of the wrist, and hold for 3 breaths. See picture 2.

3. Repeat other side.

The wrists are warmed and limbered in preparation for weight-bearing exercise. As we articulate the joints, the muscles and tendons that run from the elbows to the fingers are lubricated.

This exercise is excellent for RSI (repetitive strain injury) and great to do if you spend a lot of time at a computer.

'Articulating through the wrist'

| 1 | 2 |

Open the back of the wrist

Open the front of the wrist

Dog (Downward-Facing) Preparation

Starting in Cat position (see page 72), check your correct alignment before you begin. See picture 1.

'Keeping facial muscles relaxed and the jaw soft'

1. Inhale to prepare.

2. Exhale, draw the navel to spine and push through the palms, lifting the knees to one foot (30 cm) off the floor. Take the spine and neck with you. See picture 2.

It is essential to keep the spine and neck in one line and activate the three girdles of strength, keeping the shoulders away from the ears.

3. Inhale, release the knees to the floor.

4. Repeat 4 times.

The wrists and shoulders are strengthened in preparation for the following stronger poses.

! Caution: If you experience any pain through the wrists, you can roll a blanket or towel and place it under the heels of the palms to decrease the angle at the wrists. If this pose is still too strong, simply rest back into the Child pose.

'Strengthening, defining and toning'

1

2   Neck in line with spine

Navel to spine

Dog (Downward-Facing)

Start in Cat position (see page 72).

1. Inhale to prepare.

2. Exhale, draw navel to spine and push through the palms, coming right up onto the toes and lifting the pelvis as high as you can. See picture 1.

3. Inhale, push the heels towards the floor, coming into Downward-Facing Dog. If it feels more comfortable for you, step your feet back a couple of inches (about 5 cm). Repeat 2–10 times. See picture 2.

4. Work with lifting the tailbone high, taking the weight out of the wrists. Sense the lightness of the pose, the even pressure through the palms and the feet, and the neck soft and released. Breathe deeply as this pose uses a lot of energy.

5. Inhale, come back up onto the toes.

6. Exhale, release down into Child pose (see page 74).

Advancing it

7. Inhale, come back up on to the toes.

8. Exhale, bend the knees to hover off the floor (see picture 3).

9. Inhale back up on to the toes (see picture 1).

10. Exhale, into Downward-Facing Dog (see picture 4).

11. Inhale, release with control the forehead back onto the hand towel. Repeat all x3 then inhale and release back into Child Pose (see page 74).

! Caution: If you feel it too strong in the lower back or the back of the legs just slightly bend the knees (see picture 4); if still too strong come down and release into Child pose, then try the Right-Angle pose as an alternative (see page 94).

This pose is an inversion; the head is lower than the heart, which brings fresh blood and oxygen to the brain, oxygenating and revitalizing the mind and body, enhancing concentration. It is excellent for rejuvenating the facial muscles and brings harmony and balance to your hormonal system. The weight of the head naturally creates traction on the neck, elongating the spine, and releasing any pressure on the discs and nerves.

Downward-facing dog strengthens the diaphragm and abdominal muscles, improving digestion, respiration and circulation.

It strengthens the wrists and shoulders, and builds endurance and stamina in all three girdles of the body.

Finally, it stretches the whole back of the body from the ankles to the wrists.

1

2

Extend through the tailbone to take the weight out of the hands

Shoulders down into mid-back

Even pressure on fingers so as to broaden the palms into the floor

Outsides of the feet parallel to mat

'Strengthening
and empowering'

3

'You are as old as your
spine is flexible' J.PILATES

4

Right-Angle

Stand by a wall and place palms onto the wall at a point halfway between the shoulders and hips. With fingers evenly spread and pointing upwards.

1. Inhale to prepare.

2. Exhale, step the body back away from the wall until your body forms a right angle with your legs, making sure the feet are in line with the hips and hip-distance apart.

3. Place even pressure through the palms, activating the arms and extending through your sit bones to the back wall, elongating through the spine. Roll the shoulders outwards, broadening the mid-back, armpits facing to the floor. At the same time open the chest. This time the head does not hang, the ears remain between the arms and you lengthen out through the tailbone, creating a flat table top with your back. Again the knees can be bent if the back arches too high (or walk the hands higher up the wall) or if it is too strong on the backs of the legs.

4. Hold for 5 breaths.

5. Releasing, walk back to the wall.

As an alternative to Downward-Facing Dog, this pose is ideal for stretching the whole back of the body, in particular the backs of the legs. The hands, wrists, shoulders and arms are also stretched.

Cobra (Bhujangasana)

Start by lying on your stomach, making sure you are comfortable. You can lie over your flat pillow if you feel strain in your lower back. Place folded hand towels under the forehead, maintaining length in the neck, again sensing your neutral spinal position.

Arms are at a 90-degree angle, elbows out in line with the shoulders, and wrists in line with elbows, then just move the elbows forward and the wrists closer to each other.

1. Inhale to prepare.

2. Exhale, draw the navel up off the floor, engaging the pelvic floor muscles by placing weight into the pubic bone. Sense the stability this creates around the pelvis and the lower back.

3. Inhale, release your abdominals back to the floor. Repeat 5 times to sense how the breathing system functions against gravity in this position.

4. Exhale. As you do this slide the shoulders down away from the ears, activating the mid-back stabilizers, raise the head up but keep the gaze to the floor, neck long and lenthened. See picture 1.

5. If comfortable in your lower back, you can advance it.

6. Inhale to prepare.

7. Exhale, navel to spine, and push up onto your palms, straightening the arms. Squeeze the buttocks, activating the Thoracic girdle of strength, extend through the toes, activating the legs. Experience the pose. Breathe into it. See picture 2.

8. Hold for three breaths.

9. Inhale, release back into Child pose (see page 74).

This pose stretches the front of the body, particularly the abdominals, opening the chest and the anterior spine. It strengthens the buttocks, shoulders and arms. It is excellent for building strength and stability in the spine.

! **Caution: If you feel any strain in the lower back lie over a flat cushion.**

1

2

Chapter 12

The Total Body

This chapter focuses on stretching, strengthening and toning the whole body. The exercises add definition to the upper and lower body, building endurance and stamina in the muscles and the systems of the body. These exercises are more advanced and will give you a stronger workout.

It is vital throughout the exercises that you draw the navel to the spine and pull up on the pelvic floor muscles to activate the Abdominal and Pelvic girdles and their connection at the pelvic platform. This ensures the spine and pelvis are protected during movement. I will refer to this activation of muscles simply as 'navel to spine'. Always remember to keep the facial muscles relaxed and the jaw soft: this ensures there is no undue tension as you work.

'Sculpting yourself into shape'

Tadasana (Mountain Pose)

Tadasana is the foundation for all the other standing poses, so let's begin at the foundation of our body, the feet.

The feet are not fixed to the ground; they move with and support the body each and every day. They need to be flexible and mobile, yet strong and firm, creating an unwavering solid platform for the body. If the feet are stiff or collapsed, our entire body may suffer from imbalances and misalignments.

Stand with the feet together, ankle bones touching, the toes spread and the arches lifted. Take the time to sense your balance, feeling an evenness of pressure through the soles of your feet. Try to maintain this integrity and placement.

Now moving from the ground up we'll take our awareness to each and every part of our body. Begin by engaging the thigh muscles, gently lifting the kneecaps, being sure not to jam the knees back. Squeeze the buttocks lightly and draw the navel to the spine softly. Through this abdominal contraction the front of the body meets with the back of the body. Sense your neutral pelvis.

Inhale, hunch the shoulders up around the ears, exhale and draw them down, creating length in the neck, having the arms active beside the body, palms facing the thighs. Slightly tuck the chin, extending through the crown of your head. Use a visual of a bunch of balloons, floating and balancing the weight of the head on top of the spine.

Focus on still maintaining your foundation. Remember the feet, anchoring and grounding the body into the floor. Imagine two opposite lines of energy extending out from your center, one grounding into the earth, the other reaching heavenward. Sense the elongation through the spine, opening the spaces between the vertebrae, allowing the discs to breathe.

With a soft gaze find a point of focus directly in front of you at eye level. Alternatively close your eyes (unless you experience dizziness) and step inside yourself.

Take time to sense the breath here, becoming in touch with your center.

Now we'll begin to shift our weight from center to sense what takes place particularly in the postural (stabilizing) muscles.

> *Tadasana is the foundation for a strong body, creating a still mind and building a solid practice. It brings balance and symmetry to the body. We retreat inwards to sense our neutral spine, self, and senses, creating a neutral mind, a standing meditation.*

'Attention, without tension'

1. Slowly take your weight onto the toes, almost lifting the heels from the floor; sense the engagement of the muscles that keep you from falling. Shift your weight back to center.

2. Repeat the process, slowly taking your weight to the heels and back, moving with awareness.

3. Now repeat the same, moving from side to side, exploring the two extremes and sensing that subtle mid-point, that place where the body is completely balanced.

4. Step inside your center of balance – your natural plumb line. This is a place we do not often take the time to feel. The body feels light, weightless, elongated and relaxed. It is no effort for the body to be here.

Lateral Roll Downs

Standing in a wide stance, feet, knees, and hips in line:

1. Inhale, raise the right arm up to the side, dropping the shoulder and maintaining length in neck. Slightly bend (soften) the knees.

2. Exhale, bend the body to the left, maintaining a neutral pelvis, expanding the right ribcage towards the ceiling. See picture 1.

3. Inhale, twist the body to look towards the floor. See picture 1.

4. Exhale, release the body, allowing it to hang forwards.

5. Inhale, hold it there. See picture 2.

6. Exhale, navel to spine, uncurl the body with knees still bent, rebuilding the spine vertebra by vertebra, keeping the head and shoulders as the last to come back up to neutral. See picture 3.

7. Repeat other side. Repeat 2 times each side.

The sides of the body gain a good stretch as the ribcage and lungs are expanded during the lateral part of this exercise, helping to aerate the lungs. The spine is mobilized and limbered both in the side (lateral) flexion and when rolling up. The back and abdominal muscles are strengthened while the internal organs are massaged. The passive inversion brings a fresh supply of blood to the brain.

! **Caution: If you experience low blood pressure or dizziness take care coming out of this pose or leave it out.**

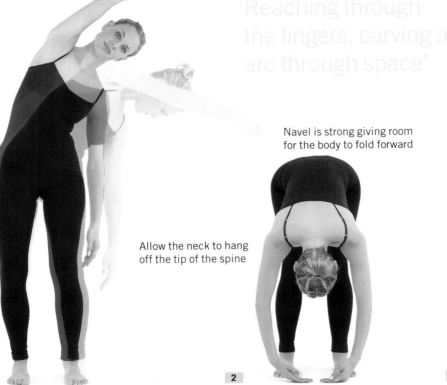

'Reaching through the fingers, carving an arc through space'

Navel is strong giving room for the body to fold forward

Allow the neck to hang off the tip of the spine

1

2

3

TOTAL BODY FLOW SEQUENCE

Each of the following poses/exercises can initially be done a few times on their own to warm the body so that you become familiar with them. They can then be linked together in a flowing sequence or be mixed and matched to suit the type of workout you require. When you feel ready you can incorporate the advanced sequences.

'Body in motion'

Arm Raises (Urdhva Hastasana)

Standing in Tadasana (see page 98):

1. Inhale to prepare, then turn the palms out, raising both arms up, taking them out to the sides and above the head; palms now facing each other, drop shoulders away from the ears, creating length in the neck.

2. Exhale, navel to spine, turn palms outward and float the arms back to your sides, perfectly co-ordinating movement and breath.

3. Repeat 5 times, warming the arms and shoulders and preparing them for the sequence.

Half Plank

From Tadasana:

1. Inhale to prepare, then take both arms up (then continuing from arm raises).

2. Exhale, navel to spine, bend forward from the hips *(if you have any back problems soften the knees)* forming a right angle with your body, still maintaining a neutral spine. Sweep the arms out to the sides in line with your shoulders as you bend. Extend through the tailbone and crown of the head.

3. Inhale, drawing abdominals in strongly, lift the body back to standing, floating the arms back up towards the ceiling, tracing an arc through space as you move.

4. Exhale, navel to spine, turn palms outward and float the arms back to your sides, into Tadasana.

5. Repeat 2 times.

Uttanasana

From Tadasana we take it a step further:

1. Inhale, raise the arms up.

2. Exhale, draw the navel to spine and bend forwards slowly, moving with control through the Half Plank. Do not be in a rush: move with awareness as you fold the body forwards. Allow the body to hang over the legs to a level that you are comfortable with and can control. Relax the arms by the sides of the body. If you need to, bend the knees, keeping them soft.

3. Hold for 2 breaths.

'Move smoothly and fluidly with intention and purpose'

Extended Uttanasana

From Uttanasana:

1. Inhale, straighten the knees (do not jam them back), elongating and ironing out the spinal curve, and creating a more horizontal extension through the spine. Come up onto the fingertips, drawing the shoulders away from the ears, creating length in the neck. Direct your gaze slightly forwards, making sure not to shorten or compress the back of the neck.

2. Hold for 2 breaths.

Dog (Downward-Facing) (see also page 92)

From Extended Uttanasana:

1. Exhale, draw navel to spine, place palms flat onto the floor, and step back into Downward-Facing Dog, with eye focus between the feet.

2. Hold for 5 breaths.

3. Inhale, with the abdominals strong, step the right foot forward followed by the left, coming into Extended Uttanasana. (*If you need to, bend the knees here.*)

4. Exhale, navel to spine, take forehead to knees into full Uttanasana.

Spinal Wave

From Uttanasana we release back to standing.

1. Inhale to prepare, with abdominals strong and knees soft. Roll the body back up, loading the correct weight of each vertebra on top of vertebra restacking the spine. Leading with the elbows the arms float back up following the movement of the body, finishing with them above the head, palms facing each other.

2. Exhale, turn palms outwards and float the arms back to the sides of the body, coming into Tadasana.

3. Notice your breath – has it changed as a result of this sequence? If you are comfortable, close your eyes for a moment, taking your awareness inside; regain your composure.

4. Repeat this sequence 5 times as it is or simply use this sequence as a warm-up for the advanced rounds.

This sequence teaches co-ordination of movement with the breath. It strengthens the muscles at the same time as lengthening them, creating a streamlined and balanced body. It incorporates passive inversion with flowing extended postures, moving the joints of the body through their full range and harmonizing the systems of the body.

Concentration and focus are enhanced, as this sequence soothes the nervous system and quietens the busy mind. All three girdles of the body are active and we learn to engage them as the body moves dynamically through the postures. This sequence builds cardiovascular fitness, enhances circulation and increases lung capacity.

'Savour the effects of these postures'

'Soft knees, soft spine'

1

2

3

ADVANCING THE SEQUENCE

Lunge

From Extended Uttanasana (see page 102):

1. Inhale to prepare, remaining up on the fingertips.

2. Exhale, draw navel to spine, stepping the right foot back into the basic lunge, extending the back leg and squeezing the buttocks, push through that heel with the knee off the floor and the kneecap lifted. Tuck the chin, slightly extending through the crown of the head and draw the shoulders down away from the ears. Find your neutral spine in this position. Find a point of focus just in front of the body.

3. Hold the lunge for 3 breaths, checking that the front knee is above that ankle with even pressure and weight distribution through the front foot; maintain the abdominal and pelvic floor contraction.

4. Exhale, push back into Downward-Facing Dog (see page 102).

5. Inhale and step back into Extended Uttanasana (see page 102).

6. Exhale, navel to spine, take forehead to knees into full Uttanasana (see page 101).

7. Inhale, release all the way back up into Tadasana (see page 98).

8. Repeat the lunge with the left leg.

The lunge strengthens the thighs, calves and ankles, creating great definition in the legs. The buttocks, arms and shoulders are toned while the connection and the co-ordination of the three girdles is promoted.

! Caution: Do not allow the pelvis to sink towards the floor: keep the hips even and level.

Warrior I (Virabhadrasana I)

From the Lunge position:

1. Inhale; using that Abdominal girdle for lift, come up into a standing lunge, front knee above ankle and back leg remaining active.

2. The arms come up in line with the ears; activate the Thoracic girdle to create length in the neck. Keep navel active and squeeze the buttocks.

3. Balance and hold for 5 breaths, finding a soft point of focus at eye level.

4. Inhale, release back down.

5. Exhale, push back into Downward-Facing Dog.

6. Inhale and step back into Extended Uttanasana (see page 102).

7. Exhale, navel to spine, take forehead to knees into full Uttanasana (see page 101).

8. Inhale, release all the way back up into Tadasana (see page 98).

9. Repeat Warrior I with the left leg.

All of the lower body, ankles, calves, thighs and pelvis are strengthened in this standing pose, creating a strong foundation for the upper body. Warrior I builds stamina, teaches balance and increases focus and concentration of the mind, building strength of will and determination.

'Strengthening, defining, and empowering'

Soft gaze point of focus

Neck and spine lengthening

Pull up on pelvic floor

Squeeze buttocks

Whole leg active

Plank

From the Lunge (see page 104):

1. Inhale, place both palms onto the floor, middle fingers pointing forwards.

2. Exhale, navel to spine, step front leg back so that both feet are back and hip-width apart, creating one long plank with the body. Extend through the heels and find your neutral spine in this pose.

3. Activate the Thoracic girdle by drawing the shoulders away from the ears, maintaining length in the neck and gaze between the hands. Hold the pose for 3 breaths.

4. Inhale, take the pelvis high coming up onto the balls of the feet.

5. Exhale, navel to spine, push the heels towards the floor into Downward-Facing Dog. Hold for 5 breaths.

6. Inhale and step back into Extended Uttanasana (see page 102).

7. Exhale, navel to spine, take forehead to knees into full Uttanasana (see page 101).

8. Inhale, release all the way back up into Tadasana (see page 98).

As an excellent full-body toner this pose builds endurance and strength in shoulders, wrists, arms and all muscles of the torso, helping to create that hourglass figure.

! **Caution: If you experience any pain through the wrists, you can roll a blanket or towel and place it under the heels of the palms to decrease the angle at the wrists. If this pose is still too strong, extend one leg back at a time.**

'Tone your torso'

Dog (Upward-Facing)

From the Plank position:

1. Inhale to prepare.

2. Exhale, navel to spine, lower the pelvis with control toward the floor, and roll the tops of the feet onto the floor.

3. Squeeze the buttocks, activate the Thoracic girdle of strength and roll the shoulders to open the chest. This helps to bring the curve into the upper back, rather than concentrating it into the lower spine. Extend through the toes, activating the legs.

Shoulder down into mid-back

Open chest

Scoop abdominals up

Squeeze buttocks

4. Hold for three breaths, curl the toes under, inhale, push up onto your toes.

5. Exhale, navel to spine, push the heels towards the floor into Downward-Facing Dog (see page 92). Hold for 5 breaths.

6. Inhale and step back into Extended Uttanasana (see page 102).

7. Exhale, navel to spine, take forehead to knees into full Uttanasana.

8. Inhale, release all the way back up into Tadasana (see page 98).

This pose stretches the front of the body, particularly the abdominals, opening the chest and the anterior spine. It strengthens the buttocks, shoulders and arms.

YOGALATES STANDING SERIES

Neutral Warrior II

From Tadasana (see page 98), step the feet 4–5 ft (1.2–1.5 m) apart, feet pointing forwards, place the hands onto the hips and sense your neutral pelvis and spine. Place even pressure through the feet and sense the balance of the body between right and left sides. Pull up lightly on the kneecaps, making sure not to jam them back, and sense the front and back of the legs working. Squeeze the buttocks gently and draw the navel toward the spine, activating a soft Abdominal girdle of strength.

Activate the Thoracic girdle, drawing the shoulders down away from the ears, creating length in the neck.

Slightly tuck the chin, extend through the crown of the head, elongating the spine. Find a soft point of focus, facial muscles relaxed, jaw soft.

Hold for 5 breaths and release back into Tadasana.

Warrior II (Virabhadrasana II)

From Neutral Warrior (see page 107):

1. Turn the left foot to the side wall, align the heel of the left foot with the arch of the right foot; notice how the right side of the pelvis rotates forward out of its neutral plane.

2. Turn the right foot slightly in to help facilitate this rotation, and allow the pelvis to stay here.

3. Inhale, lengthen the waist and raise the arms in line with the shoulders. Keep the upper torso facing to the front while maintaining the natural rotation of the pelvis.

4. Exhale, slide the shoulders down away from the ears.

5. Inhale, lengthen the waist to prepare.

6. Exhale, simply bend the left knee, slowly sinking the pelvis towards the floor and keeping the torso upright. Take your time with this. Make sure the left knee is in line with the ankle and the body is central. Sense even weight distribution between the right and left feet.

7. Inhale, tuck the chin into the throat; looking over the left fingers, find a point of focus and breathe deeply and evenly, as this pose uses a lot of energy. Hold for 5–8 breaths.

8. Inhale, release back to Neutral Warrior, neutral pelvis.

9. Repeat other side.

Warrior II invigorates the entire body, building heat and strength, increasing the circulation and heart rate. Holding this posture builds determination and will. The shoulders and arms are toned and the legs, in particular the thighs, ankles and feet, are strengthened, establishing a firm foundation and sense of grounding.

'Sense the strength of the body, and the determination of the mind'

'Feel the lines of energy extending out from your center'

Extend through opposite fingers

Pelvis naturally rotates

Pull up on the pelvic floor

Whole leg is active

Work back of foot into floor

Parsvarkonasana

Starting in Warrior II (left side):

1. Inhale, reach through the left fingers, extending the body to the left.

2. Exhale, navel to spine and take the left elbow to the left knee. Raise the right arm over the head, palm facing to the floor. Extend through the upper arm, creating one long line from fingers to the toes of the right leg. Draw the shoulders down away from the ears, creating length in the neck. Be sure to maintain activation of all three girdles and breathe into the pose. Check your alignment, left knee above left ankle.

3. Inhale, tuck the chin, and if comfortable turn the head to look to the ceiling under the right armpit; otherwise keep the head looking forwards.

4. Find a point of focus with a soft gaze, relax the jaw and facial muscles.

5. Hold for 5 breaths.

6. Inhale and release, moving through Warrior II and coming back to Neutral Warrior.

7. Repeat on the other side.

This pose stretches the sides of the body, creating length in the torso and shaping the waist. The abdominal and back muscles are strengthened. It elongates the spine, and builds endurance and stamina in the legs and lungs. The heart rate is increased and the metabolism is given a boost.

After this total-body toner, you can continue to work through the book or relax back into Savasana and continue another day.

Caution: Do not jam the back of the knee; find a balance between the front and back of the leg being active.

'Keeping the facial muscles relaxed and the jaw soft'

Chapter 13
Band Series

Yogalates uses physiotherapy exercise bands to build and lengthen the muscles of the body in a safe way throughout their correct range of movement.

The exercise band is a flexible resistance tool, which increases the intensity of stretching and strengthening the muscles. It has the added advantage of adding resistance to the workout, which helps to maintain bone density and protect you from the onset of osteoporosis.

By working with the band, you learn to work within and expand your own comfort range. The band provides support that allows you to move through and work safely within your weaker areas.

By targeting, once again, the core postural muscles, the band series stabilizes the spine, increasing muscle tone, strength and endurance, and enhances mobility, balance and co-ordination, all of which lead to overall fitness.

The band series leaves you with a feeling of elongation and lightness through the spine. The lengthening effect of these exercises helps with non-compression of the joints and spinal discs, which itself is imperative for the prevention of injury. The spine is left to move freely, optimizing its alignment and function and our posture and health.

Remember, it is vital throughout the exercises that you draw the navel to the spine and pull up on the pelvic floor muscles to activate the Abdominal and Pelvic girdles and their connection at the pelvic platform. This ensures the spine and pelvis are protected during movement. I will refer to this activation of muscles simply as 'navel to spine'. Remember always to keep the facial muscles relaxed and the jaw soft: this ensures there is no undue tension as you work.

'Creating a balanced practice, strength and flexibility. Do not sacrifice one at the expense of the other'

Bicep Curl

Sitting up tall, lengthen out of the hips. Place the feet 1–1.5 ft (30–45 cm) in front of the body, flexing them, with the toes curling towards you. Place the band around the balls of the feet and toes. Pull back on the band to sense its resistance, gauging how much is comfortable for you.

Turn your palms up to face the ceiling.

Just holding the elbows to the side of your waist, sit up tall, right out of the hips. Keep the shoulders down away from the ears. For a moment sense your neutral spine. See picture 1.

1. Inhale to prepare.

2. Exhale, navel to spine, pull back on the band; your elbows go past the waist but stay close to the body. See picture 2.

3. Inhale, release part way keeping tension on the band.

4. Exhale and repeat 10–20 times.

5. Find a soft gaze, point of focus with the eyes directly in front of you at eye level.

The Bicep Curl creates definition in the arms while strengthening the mid-back, bicep and forearm muscles.

! Caution: If you feel any tension in the neck make sure the shoulders are down, neck is long, and lessen the resistance until you are comfortable.

Band Pelvic Rock

Starting in the Bicep Curl position, keeping the elbows in at the waist:

1. Inhale to prepare.

2. Exhale, navel to spine, sense a strong contraction as you pull up on the pelvic floor muscles, tuck the pelvis under, creating a crease and fold across the waist. This causes the lower back curve to flatten, and the pubic bone to tilt towards the head.

3. Inhale and spring back up to neutral.

4. Repeat 10 times.

As you rock the pelvis, you mobilize the lumbar spine and tone the abdominal and pelvic floor muscles. The lower back also receives a stretch.

C Curve

Starting in the Bicep Curl position we advance and deepen the Pelvic Rock exercise.

1. Inhale to prepare.

2. Exhale, navel to spine, again pull up on the pelvic floor muscles, tuck the pelvis under and this time roll further down towards the floor, just to where you feel comfortable. Sense a C-shaped curve through the back of the spine.

3. Inhale, slowly release back up to neutral, keeping the abdominals in, sense how they will want to push out, but with control, keep them drawing in.

4. Exhale, this time curling like a ball over your knees.

5. Inhale, spring back up to neutral.

6. Repeat 5–10 times.

! **Caution: If you feel any tension in the neck or lower back you have come down too far. Simply release to a more comfortable level.**

Band Oblique Curl

Using the same position as for the C Curve exercise:

1. Inhale to prepare.

2. Exhale, navel to spine, again engaging the pelvic floor, tuck the pelvis under and roll to your comfortable C Curve position.

3. Hold it here, maintaining abdominal control.

4. Inhale, release band tension through the right arm only, allowing the body to come in to a slight rotation (left shoulder to right knee).

5. Exhale, drop back with control into the C Curve.

6. Repeat other side, alternating 5–10 times between each side.

7. Inhale, slowly release back up to neutral, keeping the abdominals in. Again sense how they want to push out, but keep them drawing in.

8. Exhale, this time curling like a ball over your knees.

9. Inhale, spring back up to neutral.

Full Roll Down

Starting in the Bicep Curl position (see page 112), continue into the C Curve position.

You can either have the knees bent throughout this exercise or, if your back is strong enough, straighten the legs.

1. Inhale to prepare.

2. Exhale, navel to spine, again tucking the pelvis under, this time roll all the way down to the floor, slowly and with control. See picture 1.

3. Sense the lower back first making contact with the floor, then the mid-back; as the mid-back broadens onto the floor, the lower back springs up to its neutral position.

4. The neck and head follow the rest of the spine to the floor. Relax the neck and shoulders here. See picture 2.

5. Inhale.

6. Exhale, navel to spine, tuck the chin and start to curl the head up, then slowly peel the spine back up off the floor, coming up to neutral. Again sense the abdominals as they want to push out, but keep them drawn in with control.

7. Still with the exhale, curl the body forwards over your knees, like a ball. See picture 3.

8. Inhale, spring back up to neutral.

9. Repeat 5–10 times.

The C Curve, the Oblique Curl and the Full Roll Down exercises all assist with mobilizing the spine by stretching the muscles that run (vertically) along either side of it. This stretching on the spinal column creates a nerve stretch that enhances nerve function. All three exercises work to tone the abdominal and pelvic floor muscles. The C Curve targets more the lumbar and sacral regions. The Oblique Curl targets the abdominal muscles on the sides of the body, while also activating the deep spinal rotators, aiding stability of the spine. The Full Roll Down works and mobilizes the whole spine, and with extended legs can include a stretch for the backs of the legs.

! Caution: If you are unable to roll your body back up, simply roll onto your side and push yourself back up to a seated position. Continue in this way or return to the C Curve exercise. If you feel that you run out of breath before you complete the movement, you can simply stop, take a small breath into the lungs and exhale, and continue with the movement.

Classic Hamstring Stretch

Starting in Supine Rest position we simply bend the right knee and place the band around the ball and toes of the foot.

1. Inhale to prepare.

2. Exhale; we start to extend the leg up in line with the hip.

3. Sense the resistance of the band, pull down on the band, anchor the elbows in at the waist and onto the floor, keeping the neck long and lengthened; the Thoracic girdle is active. If you feel the stretch too strongly in the back of the leg then slightly bend the knee, working to where you are comfortable, but still getting a good stretch.

4. Hold and breathe into the stretch for 5–10 breaths.

Variation
Simply draw circles with the foot up onto the ceiling, sensing the movement in the hip, trying to keep the pelvis stable. Draw small circles in one direction, increasing the size as you feel comfortable, and then reverse rotation, returning to the small circles. Repeat 10 circles in each direction.

As the name suggests, this exercise stretches the hamstrings. The 'hamstrings' are actually a muscle group, consisting of three different muscles. As you add the circle variation, you actually stretch each portion of this group as well as the inner thigh. It is great for relieving back pain and limbering up the hips, aiding hip and pelvic mobility.

'Release tension from your spine'

'Soft point of focus, gaze centered on the ceiling'

Band Single Leg (45°)

Starting in the Classic Hamstring Stretch position (see page 115):

1. Inhale, start to push up through the ball of the foot, then point the toes, isolating two different movements here. See picture 1.

2. Exhale, first drop the toes then release the foot and push through the heel.

3. Repeat this 5 times.

4. Inhale, push through the ball of the foot, hold this position, visualizing that you are standing on your tiptoes.

5. Exhale, bend the knee into the chest. See picture 2.

6. Inhale to prepare.

7. Exhale, draw the navel to spine and extend the leg out to a 45-degree angle; sense the work of the thigh and buttock muscles as the leg is held active, pushing through the ball of the foot. See picture 3.

8. Inhale slowly, with control release the leg back to the chest.

9. Repeat 10 times.

1

Push through the ball of foot

Elbows in

Keep back of pelvis anchored to floor

2

'The calf definer'

3

Band Single Leg (Straight)

Working from the Single Leg 45°, inhale, taking the leg straight up into the air, maintaining the foot position (see picture 1 opposite).

1. Exhale, navel to spine, float the leg toward the floor, hovering it just off the floor; squeeze the buttocks (see picture 4).

2. Inhale and spring the leg straight back up in line with the hip.

3. Exhale and repeat 10 times.

4. To release, hold the leg high and release the foot back into a flex position, extending through the heel and releasing the back of the ankle and leg.

5. Repeat on the left leg.

This pose is excellent for toning and shaping the calf muscles. It also strengthens the whole leg, as the front and back of the leg is kept active the whole time. It articulates the foot, which assists in pumping the blood back to the heart, increasing circulation. By using the resistance band, you get a workout as you lengthen and shorten the muscles, as you push out and as you come back in.

'The total leg and butt toner'

4

Push through the ball of the foot

Pull back on the band

No tension in neck and shoulders

Anchor elbows and back of pelvis onto floor

Band Adductor Stretch I

Starting in the Classic Hamstring Stretch position with the right leg (see page 115), place the band into the right hand and the left hand onto the left hipbone. Keep the pelvis firmly anchored into the floor, and turn the foot out away from the body.

1. Inhale to prepare.

2. Exhale, navel to spine, take the leg out to the right side of the body.

3. Tuck the chin into the throat and look over the right shoulder.

4. Hold for 5–10 breaths and breathe into the stretch.

5. Repeat with the left side.

This pose is excellent for stretching the inner thigh muscles, opening the hips and front of the pelvis.

Band Abductor Stretch II

Starting in the Classic Hamstring Stretch position with the right leg, this time place the band into the left hand and extend the right arm out to the side. Point the foot across the body.

1. Inhale to prepare.

2. Exhale, navel to spine, take the leg across the body, keeping the pelvis and both buttocks on the floor.

3. Hold it here for 5 breaths.

Twist Supine With Band

Starting in the Band Abductor Stretch II position:

1. Simply exhale and peel the pelvis off the floor, taking the leg across the body to where you are comfortable, adding a spinal rotation.

2. Hold for 5 breaths, engage the abdominals strongly, protecting the lower back and making room for the body to fold. Point through the left toes, lengthening the underside of the body.

3. Exhale, release the leg back up to center.

4. Repeat with the left side.

As you take the leg across the body, the whole outer leg gets a stretch from the ankle to the buttocks and hip. As we move further into the twist, the deep spinal rotators are activated, aiding in spinal stability.

'Mobilizing your spine,
creating freedom for movement'

Chapter 14
Dynamic Stretching

This stretching sequence prepares the mind and body for relaxation and is a vital component to your practice.

It is extremely important to stretch the body and the muscles after a workout. During exercise, a natural waste product called lactic acid is produced within the body. This lactic acid can be thought of as a thick toxic glue which, if ignored, can clog the muscles, causing muscular fatigue and soreness. Stretching the body helps to thin the glue, breaking down and removing the lactic acid, detoxifying the system, and restoring the muscles to an elastic, healthy state.

It is imperative throughout the stretches that you draw the navel to the spine and pull up on the pelvic floor muscles. This activates the Abdominal and Pelvic girdles and strengthens their connection at the pelvic platform. This ensures the spine and pelvis are protected during movement. I will refer to this activation of muscles simply as 'navel to spine'. Remember always to keep the facial muscles relaxed and the jaw soft: this ensures there is no undue tension as you work.

'Stretching to the north,
south, east and west'

Lunge (Beginners and Intermediate)

Come to kneeling on the floor, on your blankets. Check the hips, knees, and feet are in line. Beginners will need to place a chair out in front of the body. Taking hold of the chair, sense your neutral spinal alignment still.

1. Inhale to prepare.

2. Exhale, raise the right knee forward, to place the foot out in front of the body. Check that you can see your toes in front of the knee (the knee is *not* directly above the toes).

3. Exhale, tuck the pelvis under, and feel a stretch at the front of the thigh and deep into the hip. If the stretch is very mild then move deeper into the posture.

4. Inhale, lengthen the waist.

5. Exhale, navel to spine, and lunge forward towards the chair, causing the chair to slide away from you slightly, just until you feel a stretch. Squeeze the left buttock, draw the shoulders back to open the chest and slightly tuck the chin, lengthening the back of the neck. Find your balance.

6. Hold for 5 breaths.

7. Inhale, press weight through the foot into the floor and spring back up.

8. Repeat again this side, using the breath to lunge deeper into the stretch.

9. Repeat other side.

10. Release into Child pose (see page 74).

Advanced:

This time place your hands onto your hips and sense your balance, neutral pelvis and spinal alignment. It is very important to keep your balance with this exercise so as not to stress the knee.

1. Inhale to prepare.

2. Exhale, raise the right knee, placing the foot out in front of the body. Check to see if you can see your toes in front of the knee.

3. Inhale, lengthen the waist.

4. Exhale, tuck the pelvis under and lunge the body forward so the knee then sits over the ankle. If the knee passes over the foot, walk your foot further forward.

5. Squeeze the left buttock and draw the shoulders back to open the chest. Slightly tuck the chin to lengthen the back of the neck. Find your balance here.

6. Hold for 5 breaths.

7. Inhale, press weight through the foot into the floor and spring back up.

8. Repeat again this side, trying to lunge deeper with the breath.

9. Repeat other side.

10. Release into Child pose.

The quadriceps and the hip flexors at the front of the thigh and hip receive an excellent stretch in this exercise. These muscles, when tight, pull the pelvis forward, taking it out of its neutral position, causing imbalances through the spine and body, hence the importance of keeping their flexibility.

! Caution: It is very important when you lunge into this exercise to have the knee in line with the ankle; if it is forward you will stress the knee.

'Soft gaze, with point of focus directly in front at eye level'

Tuck the pelvis under

Saw Spinal Rotation Twist

Begin by sitting up tall, legs opened wide, feet 3–4 ft (1–1.2 m) apart. Try to keep the kneecaps pointing directly up towards the ceiling. If you find you are tight in the inner thigh, do not have the legs so wide.

Flex your feet and push through your heels, anchoring the back of the legs into the floor for stability.

1. Inhale, raise both arms up to the sides in line with the shoulders.

2. Exhale, draw the shoulders down away from the ears.

3. Inhale, lengthen through the spine. See picture 1.

4. Exhale, navel to spine; keeping the legs anchored and stable, twist at the waist, turning the body to face the left leg. Take your head and chest towards the left thigh. Reach your small finger towards the outside of the small toe, or as far as you feel comfortable. Hold this stretch, reaching forward and lengthening through the crown of the head. See picture 2.

5. Exhale, scoop and hollow the abdominals back to the spine.

6. Inhale, release slowly with control, just as you went into the pose.

7. Repeat other side and then alternatively 5 times.

This pose is excellent for activating the deep rotators of the spine (strengthening one side and stretching the other), aiding spinal stability and flexibility. It creates an abdominal massage, wringing every drop of impure air out of the bottom of the lungs. As you release from the twist the internal organs and discs receive a fresh supply of blood, stimulating their function, aiding in absorption of nutrients, digestion of food and the release of toxins and wastes. The lungs naturally fill up with revitalizing air. The Saw stretches the lateral muscles on the side of the spine. Worked in conjunction with the breathing system, it will help to shape and trim the waist.

1

2

'On the release of a twist the lungs naturally fill with revitalizing fresh air'

Open Chest (Baddhakonasana)

Sitting with the soles of the feet together, the knees are wide. If you need to, you can sit up onto your cushion.

1. Clasping hold of the feet, try to work the knees down towards the floor. Hold and breathe into the pose.

2. Place the hands onto the floor at your back, fingers pointing away from you; press the palms down.

3. Inhale, lengthen through the spine.

4. Exhale, work the knees down towards the floor; squeeze the shoulders back opening and breathing into the chest, expanding the lungs. Keep the navel strong and remember to pull up on the pelvic floor. You can add an eye exercise here by simply looking up to the ceiling. Watch that you do not let the head drop back as this compresses the back of the neck.

5. Inhale, release, extend the legs forward, shaking them to release the muscles.

Baddhakonasana is excellent for opening the hips, stretching the inner thighs and groin. It stabilizes the pelvis and releases any tension in the lower back. The chest and front spine are opened as the intercostals are stretched, increasing lung capacity. Fresh blood is delivered to the reproductive organs, which is excellent for PMT, menstruation and health of the prostate.

'The facial muscles are relaxed and the jaw is soft'

Squeeze shoulder blades together

Open the front of your spine and present the chest

Work the knees down to the floor

Press the soles of the feet together

Seated Garudasana

Sit with the legs out in front of the body, knees bent slightly. Place the left foot under the right leg, resting next to the right buttock. Cross the right leg over the left knee, resting up against the outer edge of the left thigh. Place both hands onto the knees and try to sink the right hip and sit bone down towards the floor. Balance here, sensing an evenness of weight distributed between the right and left sit bones, and observe your neutral spine. Sense the stretch into the buttocks and hips.

1. Inhale, extend both arms out in front, keeping the shoulders down. Place the right arm over the left (the same as the legs), bend the elbows. Try to clasp hold of the palms with the fingers, or simply place the backs of the hands together, extending through the fingers.

2. Inhale, lengthen the waist.

3. Exhale, raise the elbows high and slide the shoulders down, creating length in the neck. Sense a stretch through the back of the neck and into the mid-back.

4. Hold it here and breathe for 5 breaths.

5. Inhale, release slowly and repeat the other side.

Variation

If comfortable, on an exhale you can drop the head forward, increasing the stretch further.

This pose is excellent for stretching the deep rotators of the hips and the buttocks. The arms and shoulders also receive a strong stretch. It broadens the mid-back and the back of the pelvis, and is excellent for people who suffer with sciatica and lower back pain.

! Caution: If you find it to hard to balance you can isolate the stretch to just the legs or release the legs into a cross-legged position onto a cushion and stretch just the arms.

'Gaze soft, with point of focus directly in front at eye level'

Paschimottanasana

Sitting up out of the hips, extend the legs out in front of you and flex the feet. It is important to become aware of your pelvic alignment.

NOTE: If you feel you are sinking back into the pelvis creating that flat back shape as discussed in Chapter 5, page 30, you need to sit up on the edge of your cushion, creating more length in the waist. Work with the visual of rotating and taking the pelvis forward, lengthening out of the hips. As you bend forward the pelvis will come with you. See picture 1.

NOTE: If you find you have the sway-back type of body shape mentioned in Chapter 5, you need to tuck the pelvis under so as to flatten the excessive lower-back curve. Lift your pubic bone up towards your face. Maintain this alignment as you bend forward.

1. Place your strap around your feet, keeping your elbows bent. See picture 2.

2. Inhale, lengthen the waist and tuck the chin into your throat. Sense your neutral spine, lengthening into it by pulling back onto the strap like a lever.

3. Exhale, relax.

4. Inhale, lengthen to prepare using the strap.

5. Exhale, navel to spine, extend the body forward, not so much that you loose the natural curve of the spine by rounding it, but you will be lengthening the lower back and feeling a stretch. Maintain neutral spine. If you find you are getting a good stretch at this level stay here, otherwise:

6. Inhale, lengthen again, out of the hips.

7. Exhale, navel to spine, extend the body further forward by bending the elbows and pulling back on the strap. Fold the body to where you feel a good stretch and hold it. Do not forget your pelvic alignment: check it here and make the appropriate adjustments. Breathe into it. See picture 3.

8. Hold for 5–10 breaths.

! Caution: It is important to maintain the distance and length at the front of the body, so as not to constrict your breathing.

This pose stretches the backs of the legs, thighs, calves and ankles as well as the muscles that run (vertically) along the spine connecting the base of the skull to the back of the pelvis. Targeting the muscles which are responsible for holding the pelvis in a tucked position, (see Chapter 5), this stretch helps to reverse the flat-back body type.

Forward bends are excellent for strengthening the abdominal muscles. The action of bending forward compresses and massages the internal organs, which supports the detoxification process. On the release of a forward bend, a fresh supply of blood and nutrients circulates through the abdominal cavity, purifying and maximizing the health of the body.

'Breathe into your spine and massage your heart'

'Keeping the navel in gives room for
your body to fold,
protecting your back
while you do so'

1

2

3

Seated Twist

Sitting cross-legged on your cushions, lengthen up out of the hips, finding your neutral spinal alignment.

1. Inhale, lengthen out of the waist.

2. Exhale, rotate the body to look over your left knee. Place your right hand onto the left knee to act as a lever.

3. Inhale, lengthen again.

4. Exhale, navel to spine, twist the body, placing your left hand behind you. Take your spine and pelvis with you into the twist. See picture 2.

5. Inhale, release a little and lengthen.

6. Exhale, twist a little deeper.

7. Inhale, release a little and lengthen.

8. Exhale into a deep rotation.

9. Repeat 5 times.

10. Inhale, release and repeat the other side.

This pose is excellent for activating the deep rotators of the spine. It strengthens one side and stretches the other, aiding spinal stability and flexibility. It creates an abdominal massage, wringing every drop of impure air out of the bottom of the lungs. As you release from the twist the internal organs and discs receive a fresh supply of blood and nutrients, stimulating their function and aiding in absorption, digestion and toxic release. The lungs naturally fill up with revitalizing air. This pose also stretches the lateral muscles of the spine. Working in conjunction with the breathing system, twists help to shape and trim the waist.

'Creating that hourglass figure'

1

2

Neck Rolls

Sit up comfortably cross-legged on your cushions and find your balance. Sense the integrity of the spine and your neutral spinal alignment.

1. Inhale and, without moving the spine, allow the head to drop and release to the side, moving the right ear towards the right shoulder.

2. Holding this position, try to work the opposite shoulder down, increasing the lateral stretch through the left neck and shoulder.

3. Inhale.

4. Exhale, roll the head forward, down and around, taking the left ear towards the left shoulder. Hold it here and breathe into the stretch. See picture 1.

5. Inhale.

6. Exhale, allow the head to roll forward and down, taking the chin to the throat; pausing here, clasp the fingers at the back of the head. Slide the shoulders down and let the weight of the arms just rest here. Breathe into the stretch. See picture 2.

7. Inhale, release the arms down.

8. Exhale, tuck the chin, releasing the neck, rebuilding the cervical spine back to neutral.

This pose is excellent for stretching the neck, releasing any tension that may have arisen, particularly after the stronger poses.

'Unwind the neck, roll, limber, massage and revitalize'

1

2

Chapter 15
Relaxation – Savasana

Now that you've finished your external, physical Yogalates practice, it's time to stop and experience an equally important, but internal process. Savasana, or relaxation, is an internal workout, and it's vital to come into Savasana at the end of your practice, allowing time for the body to absorb and integrate all your hard work.

Learning to relax is part of living well, but for some, this is one of life's greatest challenges. In our busy and sometimes stressful lives, it's hard to find the time to simply stop and be. Without being aware of it we are using up huge amounts of energy which can cause an overload on the bodily systems and create exhaustion. Then mental fatigue sets in and the body becomes tired and tense, leaving it vulnerable to disease.

To counteract this we need to set aside a time each day to rejuvenate ourselves. Even as little as five minutes a day is enough time to nurture ourselves, and use relaxation to recharge the body the way nature intended, and focus the mind inwards, developing self-awareness.

There is no more reliable measure of stress and fatigue than the quality of the breath. When the body and mind are stressed, the breath is laboured – short, hectic and rough. This irregular, fragmented sound is an indication of how ill at ease we are with ourselves. As we know, we use the breath to get in touch with the body and mind and form a connection between the two. So now take some time to sense the simplicity and quality of the breath as it feeds your body, and remind yourself that breath is the essence of life. Notice the rhythm of the breath when the body is relaxed and the mind is calm, and sense how the breath flows like a smooth, even, uninterrupted, silent stream of water.

One of the most common poses in Yoga is Savasana, which translates to the Corpse pose, meaning literally to lie as still as you possibly can. No movement, no fidgeting, no restlessness – nothing but stillness. At first you may find this challenging, but I promise that as you persevere, you'll eventually find that every time you do this, you will move into a state of blissful stillness. It's this moving into stillness that integrates mind, body and spirit, leading to a calmness which we carry through our lives, and enabling us to integrate holistically into society. And the end result? Perfect peace for body and mind.

The three following postures will relax and rejuvenate. They can be used at intervals during your practice, or simply practiced by themselves. These poses are also excellent tools for receiving feedback from your body, via the action and vibration of the nervous system. So allow yourself time to listen to your body and use them as such. It's important to be warm during relaxation, as the body's metabolism slows down, and although you may feel warm from your workout, your body will cool down quickly.

Savasana

Lying long along the floor, make sure your upper body is in line with your lower body. Place your hand towel under your head and a flat pillow under the knees, to align the spine. I find that a great way to surrender into Savasana is to use the vibrations of the voice – integrating the voice with the breath.

1. So, just take a deep breath in through the nose.

2. Exhale, open the mouth and say a deep, long, slow sigh – 'AAAHHH', releasing any tensions and relaxing the body as you do so. Sense the resonating sound of your voice as it vibrates through you.

3. Repeat 3–5 times.

4. To deepen your relaxation experience, imagine you are lying in warm soft sand – and each time you exhale, imagine yourself softly sinking deeper. Allow any tension in the mind and body to simply drift away – but not so much that you fall asleep. Discipline is needed to keep the mind alert in this soft and healing state of being, as the body progressively falls into a deep, relaxed state.

5. Relax the facial muscles – the jaw, forehead and crown of the head soft, with no tension in the face.

6. As we know, it's just as important to relax the abdominals as it is to activate them. Take a deep breath in and redirect the breath down into the belly, blowing it up like a balloon. As the breath releases, allow the belly to go soft, like jelly.

7. Your body will tell you when this rejuvenating process is complete. The minimum time is at least five minutes; the maximum is up to you but try not to fall asleep. To come out of Savasana, start to deepen the breath, moving the fingers and the toes.

8. Inhale, lifting the arms up into the air.

9. Exhale, lifting them over the head to the floor behind you for a wake-up stretch, reach through the fingers and extend through the toes. Hold for a couple of breaths.

10. Inhale, lifting the arms back up.

11. Exhale, lowering the arms to the sides of the body.

12. Inhale, bend both knees and roll over onto your right side, resting in this foetal position, until you feel ready to come up.

The Yogis say, 'Always roll onto your right side in order to protect the heart.'

Savasana is refreshing and rejuvenating, creating harmony between body, mind and spirit, and regulating the blood pressure by bringing all the systems of the body into a balanced state. The period of time you spend in this pose teaches you to be tension-free yet wide awake at the same time and regulates the blood pressure by bringing all the systems of the body into a balanced neutral state.

! **Caution: It's very important to make the transition from Savasana back to your busy day as gradual as possible, so as not to agitate and shock the nervous system. Do this by bringing yourself up into a sitting position as slowly as you can. Enjoy this position for between 5 and 20 minutes.**

'Closing eyes and retreating inward'

Supported Savasana

Lying long along the floor, make sure your upper body is in line with your lower body. Place two flat pillows under your back, vertically in line with the spine, to open the chest. Put another one under the back of the knees. Rest your head onto your hand towels, positioning your head slightly higher than your chest. The arms are splayed out from the body, palms facing up to the ceiling. With each exhale, surrender into the pose, allowing the soft healing to begin.

Supported Savasana tackles one of the classic – and incorrect – postures where the shoulders roll forwards, closing the chest, guarding the heart and emotions, inhibiting the natural breathing rhythm and placing the body into an overprotective state of being. Supported Savasana reverses this protective armour, by allowing the shield to peel away, surrendering and opening the chest and front of the body into a nurturing receptive state, allowing the skin to soften and drape over the body.

'One of the best ways of learning to meditate is the journey of Savasana'

Legs Up The Wall (Viparita Karani)

Lie on your back with your legs resting up against a wall, making sure the pelvis is firmly anchored onto the floor. If you find that the pelvis is lifted, move yourself away from the wall. If you feel discomfort along the spine, lie on a blanket.

Or you can place a folded blanket under the buttocks. Place a hand towel under the head and splay the arms out by the sides of the body, palms facing to the ceiling. Lie in this position for 5–20 minutes, allowing the body to receive the rejuvenating qualities of this pose.

Legs Up The Wall is what we call a passive inversion, where the blood flows back towards the heart, working with gravity instead of against it. This releases pressure on the veins and arteries, allowing the pooled blood and fluid retention around the ankles to drain away – making this an excellent pose for people who stand on their feet all day. It also stretches the backs of the legs and lower spine, broadens the back of the pelvis and revitalizes the reproductive organs. It's great for relieving symptoms of PMS and helps to balance the bodily systems. Legs Up The Wall is an excellent pose for doing on a daily basis – and is often credited with keeping the legs young.

! Caution: If you develop any pins and needles in the feet or legs, simply bring your legs down and lie in Savasana.

'Orchestrate softness in this pose'

Supta Baddha Konasana

Place the soles of the feet together and draw them in towards you with the knees wide. You can place a cushion under each knee here, for extra comfort, and to avoid overstraining the groin. Make sure the head is higher than the chest by placing two hand towels under the head. Splay the arms to the sides, with the palms facing towards the ceiling. Rest in this position for 5–10 minutes and release yourself slowly with awareness.

This pose is a resting, reclining one. It calms and soothes the nervous system and nourishes the digestive and reproductive systems. It opens the hips, stretching the inner thigh and groin, stabilizing the pelvis and releasing any tension in the lower back. Supta Baddha Konasana opens the chest and front spine, stretching the muscles that run between the ribs (the intercostals) and increasing lung volume, helping to clear away any congestion in the sinuses and lungs. It brings fresh blood to the reproductive organs, making it excellent for PMS, menstruation problems and the prostate.

Considered to be one of the most powerful positions for regulating the menstrual cycle and balancing hormones

YOUR NEW BEGINNING

Congratulations! The relaxation that you've just done is the final part of your Yogalates practice – the conclusion to a workout which, if experienced regularly, will hone and tone your body and bring a sense of peace and calmness to the mind and spirit. What that means is that you're well on your way to a new you!

Most of us agree that exercise should be enjoyable – but also give you great results. And that's what I've strived for during the time it took me to create the Yogalates system of exercise. I believe that I've been successful in my quest for a workout which is challenging but safe, achievable yet effective and immensely therapeutic, but accessible to almost everyone.

Yogalates works on the principles of re-educating the body the way nature intended, keeping the mind and body stress free. And practiced at least three times a week, Yogalates can give you the body you've always wanted – and the mind you never knew you had.

Namaste

Chapter 16

Six Workouts

Each Yogalates program follows a sequence – from a centering phase to warm-up, a hot phase through to a cool-down, finishing with relaxation. This flow creates a safe workout with no risk of injury and ensures that maximum benefits are gained from the practice. All the phases are equally important, so always follow the sequence carefully.

As we now know, the centering phase prepares the body both mentally and physically, focusing on spinal alignment and breath. The warm-up phase increases the blood flow to the working muscles, raising their temperature so that they contract faster and more efficiently, protecting them from injury, and building the basic principles of 'the three girdles of strength'.

Now we come to the hot phase, where we experience the more dynamic and challenging exercises. Throughout the hot phase, the girdles are activated, creating the stronger, leaner body we have always wanted.

The cool-down phase, when the muscles are warm and supple, is the ideal time to stretch deeply, enhancing flexibility and preparing the mind for relaxation.

The relaxation phase is the reward – the candy at the end of your practice, designed to help your body absorb the work you have just done.

The six workouts I have designed all follow this format. Some target specific parts of the body and the others focus on the whole body. So if you have a problem area you can focus on it, using one of the shorter workouts, specially designed to fit easily into your busy day. For your convenience I have included one hour-long total-body workout which engages all major muscle groups and parts of the body. When it comes to looking and feeling good, we've learned the importance of thorough stretching. So I've included a 30-minute dynamic stretching program that, combined with the other workouts in this book, will train your body and sculpt your physique. Always remember to relax after each workout to rejuvenate and revitalize the body.

SIX PROGRAMS
Abdominal Toner – Kickstart Those Abs

Full Body Stretch (page 62)

Cushion Squeeze (page 56)

Advanced Cushion Squeeze (page 56)

Single Leg Crunch (page 82)

Oblique Curl-Up (page 59)

The Clam (page 84)

Inner Thigh Lift (page 85)

Cat (page 72)

Abdominal Roll Down Series (page 60)

Passive Back Bend (page 63)

Supine Twist (page 63)

Supported Savasana (page 133)

Upper Body – Arms and Abs Toner

Rotate and Isolate (page 68)

Wrist Rotations (page 89)

Side Push-Up (page 69)

One-Arm Push-Up (page 69)

Advanced One-Arm Balance (page 71)

Mermaid Stretch (page 70)

Plank (page 106)

Dog (Downward-Facing) Preparation (page 91)

Dog (Downward-Facing) (page 92)

Utkatasana (page 75)

Tricep Squat (page 74)

Wrist Stretch (page 90)

Shoulder Stretch (page 76)

Virasana (Forward) (page 88)

The Butt and Thigh Clencher

Full Body Stretch (page 62)

Bridge (page 80)

Bridge (Advanced) (page 80)

The Clam (page 84)

Side Leg Circles (page 85)

Bicycle (page 86)

Bicycle (Variation) (page 86)

Prone Butt Strengthener (page 87)

Virasana (Forward) (page 88)

Dog (Downward-Facing) (page 92)

Dog (hover) (page 93)

Lunge (page 104)

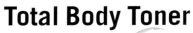
Virasana (Forward) (page 88)

Neck Roll (page 129)

Legs Up the Wall (page 134)

Total Body Toner

Lateral Roll Downs (page 99)

Tadasana (page 98)

Arm Raises (page 100)

Half Plank (page 101)

Uttanasana (page 101)

Tricep Squat (page 74)

Extended Uttanasana (page 102)

Dog (Downward-Facing) (page 92)

Spinal Wave (page 103)

Cat (page 72)

Cat and Back Extension (page 73)

Seated Garudasana (page 125)

Chest Stretch (Beginners) (page 77)

Chest Stretch (Advanced) (page 77)

Supta Baddha Konasana (page 135)

Resistance Series

Bicep Curl (page 112)

Band Pelvic Rock (page 112)

C Curve (page 113)

Oblique Curl (page 113)

Full Roll Down (page 114)

Classic Hamstring Stretch (page 115)

Band Single Leg 45° (page 116)

Band Single Leg (Straight) (page 117

Band Adductor Stretch I (page 118)

Band Abductor Stretch II (page 118)

Twist Supine with Band (page 119)

Supported Savasana (page 133)

Dynamic Stretching

Full Body Stretch (page 62)

Passive Back Bend (page 63)

Supine Twist (page 63)

Bicycle (page 86)

Seated Pelvic Rock Series (page 58)

Rotate and Isolate (page 68)

Lunge (page 104)

Dog (Upward-Facing) (page 106)

Shoulder Stretch (page 76)

Paschimottanasana (page 126)

Seated Garudasana (page 125)

Neck Roll (page 129)

Supta Baddha Konasana (page 135)

Savasana (page 132)

Appendix – Common Health Conditions and Contra-indications

	Page no	acute sacroiliac joint pain	acute sciatica	acute discs herniation	ankle problems	arthritis of jts, hands & hips	hamstring injuries	heart conditions	hernias (hiatal)	hernias (inguinal)	high blood pressure	hip & groin injuries	intercostal muscle strain	knee problems
Ab Roll Down Series	60			x		m	x							
Advanced One-Arm Balance	71			x										
Arm Raises	100												m	
Band Adductor Stretch I	118			m		m	x			x		x		
Band Abductor Stretch II	118	x				m				x		x		
Band Oblique Curl	113			x		m								
Band Pelvic Rock	112			x										
Band Single Leg	116													
Bicep Curl	112													
Bicycle	86													
Bridge	80										m			
Bridge One-Legged-Balance	81			x										
Cat	72					m								m
Cat and Back Extension	73					m								m
Chest Stretch (adv)	77			x										m
Chest Stretch (beg)	77													m
Child	74			x	m									m
Clam	84	m												
Classic Hamstring Stretch	115													
Cushion Squeeze	56												m	m
Dog (Downward-Facing)	92			m		m	m	x				x		
Dog (Upward-Facing)	106					m								
Dog Preparation	91			m		m								
Full Body Stretch	62													
Garudasana Seated	125					m								
Inner Thigh Lift	85									x		x		m
Knee Folds	55													
Knees to Chest	62												m	m
Lateral Roll Downs	99			x				x					m	
Legs Up The Wall	134													

Key:

x – Don't practice this exercise

m – Practice the beginners' position only

	Page no	lower back pain	menstruation	neck injuries	nerve impingement	pregnancy (early)	pregnancy (later)	pressure in the eyes or ears	respiratory problems	shoulder injuries	shoulder instability	sinus problems	spondylolisthesis/spondylosis & other acute spine problems	wrist problems
Ab Roll Down Series	60	x		x		x	x			m			x	
Advanced One-Arm Balance	71		m				x		m	x			x	x
Arm Raises	100			m	m					m	m			
Band Adductor Stretch I	118	x					x						x	
Band Abductor Stretch II	118	x					x						x	
Band Oblique Curl	113	x		m		x	x						x	
Band Pelvic Rock	112	x		m		x	x						x	
Band Single Leg	116	m					x							
Bicep Curl	112	m		m						m				
Bicycle	86						m							
Bridge	80	m	m	m			x	m	m			m		
Bridge One-Legged-Balance	81	x	m				x	m	m					m
Cat	72	m			m									m
Cat and Back Extension	73	m			m					m				m
Chest Stretch (adv)	77			m		x	x	x				x		
Chest Stretch (beg)	77													
Child	74	m		m			m		m			m		
Clam	84													
Classic Hamstring Stretch	115			m			x							
Cushion Squeeze	56	m					x							
Dog (Downward-Facing)	92	m						m	m	m				m
Dog (Upward-Facing)	106	m				x	x	m						m
Dog Preparation	91	m												m
Full Body Stretch	62						x			x				
Garudasana Seated	125		m						m	x	x			
Inner Thigh Lift	85						m			m				
Knee Folds	55						x							
Knees to Chest	62					x	x		m					
Lateral Roll Downs	99					x	m		m		m			
Legs Up The Wall	134				x		x	x	m					

	Page no	acute sacroiliac joint pain	acute sciatica	acute discs herniation	ankle problems	arthritis of jts, hands & hips	hamstring injuries	heart conditions	hernias (hiatal)	hernias (inguinal)	high blood pressure	hip & groin injuries	intercostal muscle strain	knee problems
Lunge (Basic)	104											x		m
Lunge Beg/Inter	122											x		m
Lying Long	31													
Neck Rolls/Stretch	129/53													
Oblique Curl-Up	59			x										
Open Chest	124				x		x					x		m
Parsvarkonasana	109			x				x			m			m
Paschimottanasana	126			x		m								
Plank	106			m				x			x			
Plank Half	101			x				m						
Prone Butt Strengthener	87													
Right Angle	94						m							
Savasana	132													
Saw Spinal Rotation	123			x								m	m	
Seated Pelvic Rock	58													
Seated Twist	128			m									m	
Shoulder Lifts	54													
Shoulder Stretch	76			x							x			
Side Leg Circles	85			m						x		x		
Side-Lying Breathing	83								m					
Side Push-Up	69			x										
Single Leg Crunch (Beg)	82			x								m		
Single Leg Crunch (Adv)	82			x								x		
Spinal Wave	103			m									m	
Supported Savasana	133													
Supta Baddha Konasana	135											x		m
Tadasana	98													
Tricep Squat	74													
Twist Supine with Band	119			x								m	m	
Utkatasana	75										m			m
Uttanasana	101			x				x			x			
Virasana (Forward)	88			x										m
Virasana (Supported)	66													m
Warrior I	105			x		m		x			x	m		m
Warrior II	107			m				x			x	m		m
Wide Knees	57											x		

	Page no	lower back pain	menstruation	neck injuries	nerve impingement	pregnancy (early)	pregnancy (later)	pressure in the eyes or ears	respiratory problems	shoulder injuries	shoulder instability	sinus problems	spondylolisthesis/spondylosis & other acute spine problems	wrist problems
Lunge (Basic)	104	m					x							
Lunge Beg/Inter	122	m					m							
Lying Long	31	m					x							
Neck Rolls/Stretch	129/53			m										
Oblique Curl-Up	59	m		m		x	x			m				
Open Chest	124	m												
Parsvarkonasana	109	m	m	m			m		m				x	
Paschimottanasana	126	x				m	x		m					
Plank	106	x	m				m		m	x			m	m
Plank Half	101	m					m						x	
Prone Butt Strengthener	87	m			m	x	x							
Right Angle	94	m								m				m
Savasana	132	m					m							
Saw Spinal Rotation	123	x			m		m						x	
Seated Pelvic Rock	58	m				x	x							
Seated Twist	128	m		m		x	x							
Shoulder Lifts	54						x							
Shoulder Stretch	76	x		x	x		x	x	m	x		x	x	
Side Leg Circles	85									m				
Side-Lying Breathing	83					x	x	x	m					
Side Push-Up	69	m		m						m				m
Single Leg Crunch (Beg)	82			m		x	x						x	
Single Leg Crunch (Adv)	82	x	m	m		x	x		m				x	
Spinal Wave	103					m			m					
Supported Savasana	123						m							
Supta Baddha Konasana	135	m					x						x	
Tadasana	98													
Tricep Squat	74													
Twist Supine with Band	119	m		m	m	x	x							
Utkatasana	75		m				m							
Uttanasana	101	x		m			m	x	m	m		x		
Virasana (Forward)	88						m			m		m		
Virasana (Supported)	66	m												
Warrior I	105	m	m				m		m	m	m		x	
Warrior II	107		m				m		m	m	m			
Wide Knees	57						x							

143

ACKNOWLEDGEMENTS:

Firstly I would like to thank Conrad Withey at Momentum Pictures for pressing that Google search button which connected the both of us in the first place. For launching the Yogalates Method internationally with such professional credibility and for having faith in my concept and vision.

My book publisher Carolyn Thorne for her calm, grounded attitude and professional energy in my somewhat hectic schedule for compiling this book.

I'd like to thank Anna Michel for her energy, her inspired insight and knowledgeable creative words; her smile, encouragement and support when my mind was tired from writing this book.

Lisa Finkeneaur for her support, passion and dedication to the Yogalates method. To thank her for the time spent in compiling and illustrating the Yogalates training manual with me which led to the development of this book and for her fine editing skills.

Deborah Dooley, for her contribution to the creative writing in the introduction.

To my daughter Crystal for modelling along side mum, which I will cherish forever.

Amber Parry for her professional energy and time in modelling for the book.

Michael Travers for his brilliant perception, ability and skill in interpreting the movement of Yogalates within the human body in exactly the way I envisage and feel it.

To develop a method, patent the name Yogalates in Australia, then turn it into a government accredited training course; run a registered training organization, write and develop a training manual and make two videos is one thing. But to turn around and write a book in the time I had was a daunting task. I have never been one to let opportunity pass me by though. So a big thank you to everyone involved for making it all possible and having faith in my vision and revolutionary method. Above all to my husband Mark for being the backbone of the Yogalates method.

BIOGRAPHY

Louise Solomon was injured in a beginners' Yoga class to the point that she could not continue the practice. She was then introduced to the Pilates method and spent two and a half years practicing and teaching Pilates. During this time she recognized what was missing from the instruction of her previous yoga class (core stabilization). However, she very much missed the ambience of the Yoga room, the meditation and pranayama techniques which are hugely beneficial in maintaining a healthy central nervous system. It was then that she went back to the Yoga practice and started to develop the fusion between the two techniques of Pilates and Yoga. She decided to make Pilates more accessible for the general public and started the fusion of Yoga and Pilates in classes. Great support followed and a network of people and practitioners sprung up. The journey of Yogalates had begun.

Over the next decade she continued exploring this newly created method developing a lot of work in the studio for public classes, and also teaching sessions to physiotherapists.

She has taught and trained internationally through the USA and the UK as an accredited trainer in Yoga and Pilates. Louise conducts a registered training organization to accredit students in the Yogalates method. Yogalates is now into its fourth year of teacher training and the Yogalates Training Academy Australia is the only training course in the world run to this high degree and accredited government standard of this unique fusion technique.

Louise currently lectures at the Southern Cross University for the School of Exercise Science & Sport Management in Core Stability for the prevention of injury and rehabilitation. Keeping abreast of the latest information and scientific research in body/functional movement is the key to the Yogalates method, bridging the gap between the eastern and western form of body work. Yogalates is ever evolving and is updated accordingly.

Yogalates Training Academy Australia

Runs annual 6.5 months
Certified IV training courses
Full Time Austudy approved
Registered for International Student Visas
Check web for general information and training in the UK and USA
www.yogalates.com.au
info@yogalates.com.au
Student visas are available

STOCKISTS

Resistant training bands available in the UK from 4my Way of Life
Mail order: 0870 241 5471
Email: sales@4mywayoflife.com
Website: www.4mywayoflife.com
Stores: Flagship Store, Fulham Island, 13–15 Jerdan Place, Off Fulham Broadway, London, SW6 1BE;
7 Park Street,Leamington Spa, Warwickshire,CV32 4QN

USA: Creative Health Products
7621 East Joy Road
Ann Arbor, Michigan 48105
Tel: Freephone – 1 800 742 4478
E-mail: sales@chponline.com
Website: www.chponline.com
and in Australia/New Zealand
order via Louise Solomon's website